CAMBRIDGE LIBRARY COLLECTION

Books of enduring scholarly value

Printing and publishing history

The interface between authors and their readers is a fascinating subject in its own right, revealing a great deal about social attitudes, technological progress, aesthetic values, fashionable interests, political positions, economic constraints, and individual personalities. This part of the Cambridge Library Collection reissues classic studies in the area of printing and publishing history that shed light on developments in typography and book design, printing and binding, the rise and fall of publishing houses and periodicals, and the roles of authors and illustrators. It documents the ebb and flow of the book trade supplying a wide range of customers with products from almanacs to novels, bibles to erotica, and poetry to statistics.

Fitzwilliam Museum McClean Bequest

Frank McClean (1837–1904) was not only an astronomer and pioneer of objective prism spectrography, but also an accomplished and systematic collector of art, books and manuscripts. McClean's collections, which were left to the Fitzwilliam Museum, Cambridge, on his death, were at that time the most notable bequest since the Museum's foundation. The fifteenth- and sixteenth-century printed books in his bequest, most of them produced in continental Europe, are described here in detail, with bibliographical descriptions and information on their provenance. Illustrated books are listed separately. The author of the catalogue, Charles Edward Sayle (1864-1924) was an erudite and popular librarian whose career was devoted to cataloguing and editing rare books in the University of Cambridge. His obituary praised him as 'a fine example of the type of man who likes to catalogue things in the right order.'

Cambridge University Press has long been a pioneer in the reissuing of out-of-print titles from its own backlist, producing digital reprints of books that are still sought after by scholars and students but could not be reprinted economically using traditional technology. The Cambridge Library Collection extends this activity to a wider range of books which are still of importance to researchers and professionals, either for the source material they contain, or as landmarks in the history of their academic discipline.

Drawing from the world-renowned collections in the Cambridge University Library, and guided by the advice of experts in each subject area, Cambridge University Press is using state-of-the-art scanning machines in its own Printing House to capture the content of each book selected for inclusion. The files are processed to give a consistently clear, crisp image, and the books finished to the high quality standard for which the Press is recognised around the world. The latest print-on-demand technology ensures that the books will remain available indefinitely, and that orders for single or multiple copies can quickly be supplied.

The Cambridge Library Collection will bring back to life books of enduring scholarly value (including out-of-copyright works originally issued by other publishers) across a wide range of disciplines in the humanities and social sciences and in science and technology.

Fitzwilliam Museum
McClean Bequest

*Catalogue of the Early Printed Books
Bequeathed to the Museum by Frank
McClean, M.A., F.R.S.*

CHARLES E. SAYLE

CAMBRIDGE
UNIVERSITY PRESS

CAMBRIDGE UNIVERSITY PRESS

Cambridge, New York, Melbourne, Madrid, Cape Town, Singapore,
São Paolo, Delhi, Dubai, Tokyo

Published in the United States of America by Cambridge University Press, New York

www.cambridge.org
Information on this title: www.cambridge.org/9781108007832

© in this compilation Cambridge University Press 2009

This edition first published 1916
This digitally printed version 2009

ISBN 978-1-108-00783-2 Paperback

FITZWILLIAM MUSEUM

McCLEAN BEQUEST

CAMBRIDGE UNIVERSITY PRESS
C. F. CLAY, Manager
London: FETTER LANE, E.C.
Edinburgh: 100 PRINCES STREET

New York: G. P. PUTNAM'S SONS
Bombay, Calcutta and Madras: MACMILLAN AND CO., Ltd.
Toronto: J. M. DENT AND SONS, Ltd.
Tokyo: THE MARUZEN-KABUSHIKI-KAISHA

FITZWILLIAM MUSEUM

M^CCLEAN BEQUEST

CATALOGUE

OF THE

EARLY PRINTED BOOKS

BEQUEATHED TO THE MUSEUM
BY FRANK M^CCLEAN, M.A., F.R.S.

BY

C. E. SAYLE, M.A.

Cambridge :
at the University Press
1916

PREFACE

THIS volume completes the series of catalogues of the
McClean Bequest. The *Descriptive Catalogue of the Manuscripts* by Dr M. R. James, and the Catalogue of the Mediaeval
Ivories, Enamels, Jewellery, Gems and Miscellaneous Objects,
by O. M. Dalton, appeared in 1912. In the first of these will
be found a biographical notice of the generous benefactor Frank
McClean, M.A., F.R.S. (1837–1904), to whom the Museum is indebted for early printed books here described. In order to make
this Catalogue more complete descriptions of the other Incunabula
in the Museum have been added in an Appendix.

A List of the Fifteenth-Century Printed Books bequeathed by
Mr McClean was printed in 1906, by Mr Stephen Gaselee, now
Pepysian Librarian at Magdalene College. This has been of
great assistance. I am also indebted to Mr S. C. Cockerell, the
present Director of the Museum, for a merciless reading of the
proofs and making innumerable and invaluable suggestions.

The careful rubbings which are reproduced in plate 6 were
made by Mr W. E. Rider, Principal Assistant at the Museum.

C. E. S.

31 *August* 1916.

TABLE OF CONTENTS

ITALY

APPENDIX

DESCRIPTION OF THE PLATES

LIST OF AUTHORITIES CITED

Allgemeine Deutsche Biographie. Leipzig. 1875 etc. 8°.
Audin de Rians (S. L. G. E.). Poesie di Ieronimo Savonarola. Firenze. 1847. 8°.

Baudrier (H.). Bibliographie Lyonnaise. 7 tom. Lyon. 1895 etc. 8°.
Bohatta (H.). Bibliographie der Livres d'Heures. Wien. 1900. 8°.
Bourdillon (F. W.). The Early Editions of the Roman de la Rose. (Bibliographical Society. Monograph xiv.) London, 1906.
British Museum. Catalogue of Books printed in the xvth Century. London, 1908 etc. *In progress.*
—— Catalogue of Books in the Library of the British Museum, printed in England, Scotland and Ireland and of Books in English printed abroad, to the year 1640. 3 vols. London, 1884.
Brunet (J. C.). Manuel du Libraire. 6 vols. Paris, 1860–1865. Supplément, 2 vols. 1878–1880. Dictionnaire, 1 vol. 1870.
Brussels. Bibliotheca Hulthemiana. 6 vols. Gand. 1836—7.

Cambridge University Library. Early English Printed Books, 1475–1640. 4 vols. and Appendix. 1900–1907.
Campbell (M. F. A. G.). Annales de la typographie néerlandaise au xvᵉ Siècle. La Haye. 1874. Suppléments, 1880–1884.
Chawner (G.). A List of the Incunabula in the Library of King's College, Cambridge. Privately printed. Cambridge, 1908.
Claudin (A.). Histoire de l'Imprimerie en France au xvᵉ et au xviᵉ Siècle. 3 vols. Paris, 1900–1904.
Clement (David). Bibliothèque curieuse historique et critique. 9 vols. Göttingen, 1750-1760.
Cockerell (S. C.). Some German woodcuts of the Fifteenth Century. Hammersmith. 1897.
Colomb de Batines (Paul). Bibliografia Dantesca. 2 vols. Prato, 1845-1846.

Conway (W. M.). The Woodcutters of the Netherlands in the Fifteenth Century. Cambridge, 1884.

Copinger (W. A.). Supplement to Hain's Repertorium Bibliographicum. 2 parts (3 vols.). London, 1895–1902.

—— Incunabula Biblica. London, 1892.

Crawford (Earl of). Bibliotheca Lindesiana. Collations and Notes, no. 3. London, 1884.

Davies (Hugh William). Bernhard von Breydenbach and his journey to the Holy Land. London, 1911.

Delambre (J. B. J.). Histoire de l'astronomie du moyen âge. 3 vols. Paris, 1819.

Denis (M.). Wiens Buchdruckergeschicht bis 1560. Wien, 1782.

Dibdin (T. F.). Bibliotheca Spenceriana. 4 vols. and Supplement. London, 1814–1822.

—— Introduction to the knowledge of the most rare and valuable editions of the Greek and Roman Classics. Ed. 4. London, 1827.

Didot. Nouvelle Biographie Universelle. 45 vols. Paris, 1852–1866.

Duff (E. G.). Notes and Collations. Edinburgh Bibliographical Society. Vol. IX. p. 21 etc.

Essling (Prince d'). Les Livres à Figures Vénitiens de la fin du xvᵉ Siècle et du commencement du xviᵉ. 3 parties (5 tomes). Florence, 1907–1914.

Falkenstein (K.). Beschreibung der K. öff. Bibliothek zu Dresden. 1839.

Fuster (J. Pastor). Biblioteca Valenciana.

Graesse (J. G. T.). Trésor de livres rares et précieux. 6 vols. and Suppléments. Dresde, 1859–1869.

Guigard (J.). Nouvel armorial du Bibliophile. 2 vols. Paris, 1890.

Haebler (Konrad). Bibliografía Ibérica del Siglo xv. La Haya, 1903.

—— The Early Printers of Spain and Portugal. (Bibliographical Society. Monograph IV.) London, 1896.

Hain (L.). Repertorium Bibliographicum. 4 vols. Tübingen, 1826–1838.

Herbert (W.). Typographical Antiquities. 3 vols. London, 1790.

Hoskins (E.). Horae Beatae Mariae Virginis. London, 1901.

Houzeau (J. C.) et A. Lancaster. Bibliographie générale de l'Astronomie. 2 vols. Bruxelles, 1880–1882.

Huth (H.). A Catalogue of the Printed Books, Manuscripts, Autograph Letters, and Engravings, collected by H. Huth. 4 vols. London, 1880.

Kaestner (A. G.). Geschichte der Mathematik. 1796. 8°.

Koch (T. W.). Catalogue of the Dante Collection presented by W. Fiske. (Cornell University Library.) 2 vols. Ithaca, New York. 1898–1900.

Lacombe (P.). Livres d'Heures imprimés au xvᵉ et au xviᵉ Siècle, conservés dans les bibliothèques publiques de Paris. Paris, 1907.

Lechi (L.). Della tipografia Bresciana nel secolo decimoquinto. Brescia, 1854.

Linnig (B.). Bibliothèques et ex-libris d'amateurs belges aux xviie, xviiie, et xix Siècles. Paris, 1906.

Lippmann (F.). The Art of Wood Engraving in Italy in the Fifteenth Century. London, 1888.

Litta (Pompeo). Celebri Famiglie Italiane. 187 Dispense. Milano, 1819–1875.

Macfarlane (J.). Antoine Vérard. (Bibliographical Society. Monograph VII.) London, 1899.

Morgan (J. P.). Catalogue of manuscripts and early printed books. 3 vols. London, 1907.

Murray (C. Fairfax). Catalogue of a collection of Early German Books in the Library of C. F. Murray. Compiled by H. W. Davies. 2 vols. London, 1913.

—— Catalogue of a collection of Early French Books in the Library of C. F. Murray. Compiled by H. W. Davies. 2 vols. London, 1910.

Muther (R.). Die deutsche Bücher-illustration der Gothik und Frührenaissance. 2 Bde. München, 1884.

Panzer (G. W.). Annales typographici. 11 vols. Norimbergae, 1793–1803.

—— Annalen der älteren deutschen Litteratur. Nurnberg, 1788. 4°.

Pellechet (M.) et M. L. Polain. Catalogue général des Incunables des Bibliothèques Publiques de France. Paris, 1897. *In progress.*

Perez Pastor (C.). La Imprenta en Toledos. Madrid, 1887.

Proctor (Robert). An Index to the Early Printed Books in the British Museum. With notes of those in the Bodleian Library. 2 vols. 1898.

Quaritch (B.). Contributions towards a Dictionary of English Book-Collectors. 12 parts. London, 1892–1899.

Redgrave (G. R.). Erhard Ratdolt and his work at Venice. (Bibliographical Society. Monograph I.) London, 1894.

Reichling (D.). Appendices ad Hainii-Copingeri Repertorium Bibliographicum. 6 Fasciculi, Supplementa et Indices. Monachii, 1905–1914.

Renouard (A. A.). Annales de l'imprimerie des Estienne. Ed. 2. Paris, 1843.

Renouard (Ph.). Bibliographie des impressions et des œuvres de Josse Badius Ascensius. 3 vols. Paris, 1908.

Rietstap (J. B.). Armorial général. Éd. 2. 2 vols. Gouda, 1884.

Salvá y Mallen (Pedro). Catalogo de la Biblioteca de Salvá. 2 vols. Valencia, 1872.

Sandars (S.). An annotated list of books printed on vellum to be found in the University and College Libraries at Cambridge. (Cambridge Antiquarian Society.) Cambridge, 1878.

Schmidt (C.). Jean Grüninger. (Répertoire Bibliographique Strasbourgeois. I.) 1893.

Schreiber (W. L.).   Manuel de l'amateur de la gravure sur bois et sur métal au
    xvᵉ Siècle.   8 vols.   Berlin, 1891–1900.
Schorbach (K.) and M. Spirgatis.   Bibliographische Studien zur Buchdrucker-
    geschichte Deutschlands.   Heinrich Knoblochtzer.   Strassburg, 1888.
Smith (D. E.).   Rara Arithmetica.   Boston, 1908.

[Van Praet (J. B. B.).]   Catalogue des livres imprimés sur vélin.   8 vols.   1822–
    1828.
Voulliéme (E.).   Der Buchdruck Kölns bis zum Ende des fünfzehnten Jahr-
    hunderts.   Bonn, 1903.

Weale (W. H. J.).   Catalogus Missalium ritus Latini.   Londini, 1886.
Willems (A.).   Les Elzevier.   Bruxelles, 1880.
Winsor (Justin).   A Bibliography of Ptolemy's Geography.   (Bibliographical
    Contributions.   No. 18.)   Cambridge, Mass., 1884.
Woolley Facsimiles.   Photographs of fifteenth-century types.   [By G. Dunn.]
    1899–1905.

GERMANY

MAINZ

PETER SCHÖFFER (1457)

1. THOMAS AQUINAS. Summa secunda secundae partis.
6 March 1467. Large F⁰.

Ed. Pr.
Description in BM.Catalogue.
Collation (written signatures) a–e^{10} f^{12} g–k^{10} l–n^8 o–t^{10} v^6 x–z^{10}, 9^{10} A^{10} B^6
258 leaves.
405 × 300 mm. Parti-coloured initials, red and blue on the first page,
chapter initials numbered in contemporary hand, the rest in plain red
or blue.
Binding. Dark blue morocco, elaborate gold tooling and edges, by
Bozerian le Jeune.
Provenance. MS. inscription on first page: 'Ad usum ff. inclusorum
S. Mariae ad arborem in Cliura 1635.' Payne & Foss 1829. Syston
Park (1884), and Henry White (1902), with bookplates.
Hain *1459. Proctor 83. BM.Catalogue I. 24.

2. VALERIUS MAXIMUS. Facta et Dicta. 14 June 1471.
Small F⁰.

Description and *collation* in BM. Catalogue and Morgan Catalogue.
275 × 198 mm. Crudely rubricated, yellow initial strokes.
MS. leaf inserted containing notes (qu. by Askew?) relating to no. 50 bound
with this.
Binding. Red morocco (saec. XVIII).
Provenance. Askew (1775). Payne and Foss 1828. Syston Park (1884).
HC. *15774. Proctor 95. BM.Catalogue I. 27. Morgan I. 15 (no. 23).

3. GRATIANUS.   Decretum cum glossis Bartholomei Brixiensis.
13 August 1472.   Largest Fº.

> *Description* and *collation* in BM.Catalogue.   Last leaf of Vol. II (blank) gone.
>
> 482 × 335 mm.   On vellum.   2 vols.   Plain initials in blue or red.   On the first leaf is a finely executed Venetian initial H composed partly of a green winged dragon, on a blue ground.   At the foot of the page are the arms of the original owner (azure, a lion rampant surmounted by a crown or, grasping a cross gules), with two cherub supporters on a crimson ground, holding cornucopias.   These are the arms of Simonetta   See Litta *Celebre Famiglie.*
>
> *Binding.*   Italian red morocco with gold border, and a light blue label (saec. XVIII), agreeing with no. 4.
>
> *Provenance.*   Simonetta (ab. 1472).   Count Louis Apponyi[1] (1892), lot 535.
>
> HC. *7885.   Proctor 99.   BM.Catalogue I. 29.   Cf. Van Praet II. 2, v. 367.   Inventaire, p. 69.

4. GREGORIUS IX.   Nova compilatio decretalium cum glossa Bernhardi Bottoni.   23 November 1473.   Largest Fº.

> *Description* in Hain, and BM.Catalogue.
>
> *Collation* [a–c^{10} d^6 e^4 (+1) f–h^{10} ik^6 lm^{10} n^8 o^{10} (+9*) pq^{10} r^8 s^6 (+1) t–x^{10} y^6 z^6 (+1) & 9 A^{10} B^8 C^6 DE^{10} F^8 (+1) G–I^{10}].   4 pinholes.
>
> 470 × 335 mm.   A miniature at the beginning of Book I.   The Pope in a green cope is seated on a violet throne.   On our right four cardinals.   The spaces before Books II–V are blank (cf. BM.Catalogue).   White vine capital on first leaf.   Plain red initials throughout.
>
> Some marginal notes.
>
> *Binding.*   Brown morocco sides, rebacked in red morocco, with light blue labels agreeing with no. 3.
>
> *Provenance.*   The initials of an early Italian owner 'A. L.' at foot of the first leaf, with intermediate arms or device cut out.   Count Louis Apponyi (1892), lot 536.   Leighton, no. 2270.
>
> HC. *7999.   Proctor 103.   BM.Catalogue I. 30 (first copy).

5. TURRECREMATA (JOHANNES DE).   Expositio Psalterii.
11 Sept. 1474.   Fº and 4º.

> *Description* in Hain, BM.Catalogue, and Morgan Catalogue.
>
> *Collation* in BM.Catalogue and Morgan Catalogue.

---

[1] Apponyi Library.   See a short note on this prefixed to the sale catalogue of Messrs Sotheby.

291 × 206 mm.   Plain rubrication.   The initial B on the first leaf has a
   decorative background in brown ink.   The text-capitals touched with red.
Binding.   Blue morocco with gold tooling; gilt edges (saec. XVIII).
Provenance.   Sunderland (1883), and Henry White (1902), with bookplates.
Hain *15698.   Proctor 105.   BM. Catalogue I. 31.

6.   HORBORCH (GULIELMUS).   Decisiones novae Rotae Romanae.   3 January 1477.   Fº and 4º.

Description in Hain, cf. BM.Catalogue.
Collation: Part 1 [a⁶ b⁸⁺¹ (b 1 gone) c–h¹⁰ i¹² kl⁸ m–o¹⁰ p⁸ (8 blank gone)].
   Part 2 as in BM.Catalogue.
316 × 236 mm.   This copy is misbound, the first quire being placed at the
   end of the first part.   Sig. n–p are bound as in Hain, not as in BM.
   description.   Paragraph marks in blue or red.   Some marginal notes.
Binding.   Black half-morocco, paper sides.
Provenance.   Royal Society, 'Ex dono Henrici Howard Norfolciensis,' with
   bookplate (1872).   'No. 3225' in some catalogue.
Hain *6047.   Proctor 112.   Cf. BM.Catalogue I. p. 33.

7.   CHRONIK DER SACHSEN.   6 March 1492.   Small Fº.

In Lower Saxon dialect.   By Conrad Botho.
Description in Hain, BM.Catalogue.   Woodcuts.
Collation in BM.Catalogue.   284 leaves.
274 × 194 mm.   Wants a 1, k 8, A 8, G 4 and 5, and M⁸ N⁴ (17 leaves).
Binding.   Modern half-vellum.
Provenance.   Inscription by Joachim Negelein, the Lutheran theologian of
   Nürnberg, in 1740.   'Submisse obtulit.'
HC. *4990.   Proctor 130.   BM.Catalogue I. 37.   Morgan I. 27 (no. 33).
   Muther 638.   Schreiber 3531.

8.   AUGUSTINUS.   De vita Christiana.   [Ab. 1470–1475.]   4º.

Description in Hain, BM. Catalogue.
Collation in BM. Catalogue.
201 × 142 mm.   Plain capitals and initial strokes in red.
Wants the last leaf (blank).
Some contemporary marginal annotations.
Binding.   Olive morocco with blind tooling and gilt edges by Thompson
   of Paris.
Provenance.   A library book stamp 'MJJM' on leaf 17 verso.   No. 2791
   in a London auction catalogue after 1887.
Hain *2093.   Proctor 135.   BM.Catalogue I. 37.

ERHARD REUWICH (1486)

9. BREYDENBACH (BERNHARD VON).   Reise ins heilige Land.
21 June 1486.   Small F⁰.

First German edition.
Description in Hain, BM.Catalogue.
Collation [ab⁸ (+six folding sheets) c–m⁸ n⁶ (+one folding sheet) A–F⁸].
The early collator of this and the copy in the Cambridge University
Library reckoned the six folding sheets between b and c as three quires,
the maps having been mounted.   His collation is a–b⁸ ċ–e² (folding
sheets) f–p⁸ q⁶ r² (folding sheet) s–y⁸.
303 × 220 mm.   Not rubricated.
Binding.   Brown morocco binding, with blind tooling, by Rivière and Son.
Provenance.   Not known.
Hain *3959.   Proctor 157.   BM.Catalogue I. 44.   H. W. Davies.
Bernhard von Breydenbach, p. 9.   Schreiber 3630.

STRASSBURG

JOHANN MENTELIN (1461)

10. CHRYSOSTOMUS.   Homiliae super Matthaeum.   Not after
1466.   Small F⁰.

Description in Hain, BM.Catalogue.
Collation in Hain-Copinger.   Fol. 128 cut away.
288 × 210 mm.
The initial letter on the first page contains the inscription 'C · VII · P · M ·';
and the arms of Clement VII are blazoned on the last page.   These are
modern forgeries.
Rubricated.   Plain red initial letters and head lines.   Text capitals touched
in red.   A few marginal notes in a contemporary hand.
Binding.   Modern maiolesque, wholly· gilt, with the arms of Pope
Clement VII, in colour, in the centre of each board.   Metal clasps and
corner knobs ; the lower clasp gone.   Two leaves of a breviary of the
fifteenth century have been used as end-papers.
Provenance.   Not recorded.
HC. *5034.   Proctor 197.   BM.Catalogue I. 51.

11. AUGUSTINUS. De civitate dei. Not after 1468. Large F°.

First edition printed in Germany.
Description in Hain, BM. Catalogue.
Collation in BM. Catalogue.
397 × 290 mm. The large decorative initials handsomely executed in red,
with rubrication throughout. The initials at the beginning of Books XII
and XIV contain the date '1471,' that of Book XIII the name of the
rubricator (or owner?) 'P. Wolf.' Initial strokes.
Contemporary marginal annotations.
Binding. Russia with the Wodhull bookstamp. With no. 12.
Provenance. The first leaf contains the superscription 'Sum ex bibliotheca
Joannis Christophori Rosae. Anno 1586,' followed by 'Ad Bibliothecam
F. F. Min. Con. S. Franc. Ratisbonen.' Wodhull (1886), bought by him
at 'Payne's sale' and dated 5 Jan. 1795.
Hain *2056 (1). Proctor 201. BM.Catalogue I. 52.

12. AUGUSTINUS. Commentarium Thomae Valois et Nicolai
Triveth super libros Augustini De Civitate Dei. [Not after 1468.]
Large F°.

Description in Hain, BM.Catalogue.
Collation. B.M.Catalogue.
397 × 290 mm. Rubrication at beginning: 'Expositio fratris Thomae Anglici
ordinis praedicatorum' etc. See D.N.B. s.v. Jorz.
Binding. With no. 11.
Provenance. Ibid.
Hain *2056 (2). Proctor 202. BM.Catalogue I. 52.

13. AUGUSTINUS. De arte praedicandi. [About 1468.]
Small F°.

Description in Hain, BM.Catalogue.
Collation in BM.Catalogue.
272 × 187 mm. Wants last leaf blank.
Parti-coloured initial H at beginning of text. Paragraph marks in red and
blue alternately. A few late marginal notes.
Binding. Modern red half-morocco with paper sides.
Provenance. Bought from J. and J. Leighton.
Hain *1955. Proctor 218. BM.Catalogue I. 52.

14. AUGUSTINUS. Confessiones. [Not after 1470.] Small F°.

Description in Hain, BM.Catalogue.
Collation in BM.Catalogue.

285 × 210 mm.

The first leaf has a scroll of leaf and fruit spray on two margins, and the arms of Buxheim at foot in colour. The two initials on this page are in plain gold on plain blue or green background. The rest of the capitals and the initial strokes in plain red.

Binding. Original white leather with five stamps, consisting of the legend 'Meister,' a dog, an upright on a scroll, a quatrefoil, and a large knot. Original metal clasps.

Provenance. Bought from J. and J. Leighton.

The Buxheim bookplate has been removed from the fly leaf, but the inscription still remains:

Liber Cartusiensis in Buchshaim prope Memmingen
proveniens a confratre nostro domino Hilprando Brandenberg
de Bibraco / continens librum Confessionum beati Augustini.
Oretur pro eo et pro quibus desiderauit.

Hain *2030. Proctor 205. BM.Catalogue I. 54.

15. VINCENTIUS BELLOVACENSIS. Speculum Historiale. 4 December 1473. Large F°.

Four volumes. First dated edition.

Description in BM.Catalogue, Copinger.

Collation in BM.Catalogue. But in Vol. III, sig. aa contains 9 leaves.

470 × 325 mm. Vol. I wants first and last leaves (both blank). Vol. II wants last leaf (blank). Vol. IV the same.

The large capitals at the commencement of Books I–XVI, contained in Volumes I and II, are finely executed in red with green filigree work or blue with red filigree work. Those in the remaining volumes though rubricated were never finished.

Ordinary capitals in plain red or blue. Initial strokes in red.

Vol. I has inscription on the first leaf 'De libris Rev^di magistri Conradi Hebenhamer Orate deum pro eo' at top and 'Conventus Landeshutani Ord. F. F. Praedi.' at foot. The second inscription is repeated at the end of Vol. II.

Compositors' signatures[1] printed by hand in each volume. Vol. I 'd' throughout, II 'a,' III 'b,' IV 'c.'

Binding. Half-calf, with monogram on back with coronet of a marquis.

Provenance. Conrad Hebenhamer. Landshut.

BM.Catalogue I. 57. Proctor 212. Copinger 6246.

---

[1] Compositors' signatures. For another example of these signatures cf. B.M.Catalogue I. 57 (IC. 568). Henry Bradshaw worked at this subject in September 1877, and has left notes (F. Jenkinson, MS. transcript).

16. ISIDORUS. Etymologiarum Libri xx. [About 1473.]
Large F°.

Description in Hain, BM.Catalogue.
Collation in BM.Catalogue.
390×277 mm.
The first large capital in red and blue. The rest in plain blue or red.
  Initial strokes red. Woodcut diagrams.
Binding. Half-pigskin (saec. XVIII).
Provenance. Bought from J. and J. Leighton. No. 1026 in some sale.
HC. *9270. Proctor 227. BM.Catalogue I. 57. Schreiber 4267.

17. ALBERTUS MAGNUS. De laudibus beatae Mariae Virginis.
[About 1477–8.] Large F°.

Description in Hain, BM.Catalogue.
Collation in BM.Catalogue.
363×264 mm. Wants two blank leaves at end.
Plain initials, and initial strokes in red.
Binding. Brown morocco, with rich blind tooling, in imitation of the
  bindings of the fifteenth century by J. and J. Leighton.
Provenance. Bought of J. and J. Leighton (1905 Catalogue, no. 62).
Hain *467. Proctor 228. BM.Catalogue I. 59.

THE 'R' PRINTER (1464–1473)
ADOLF RUSCH

18. PETRARCA. De contemptu mundi. [Not after 1473.]
Small F°.

Ed. Pr.
Description in Hain, BM.Catalogue.
Collation in BM.Catalogue.
278×206 mm.
The first initial letter parti-coloured in blue and red ; capitals and initial
  strokes in red.
Binding. Plain red morocco with gold rules (eighteenth century).
Provenance. La Vallière (1783), no. 1306. No. 2433 in the collection of
  a later owner. No. 117 in some subsequent sale.
Hain *12800. Proctor 231. BM.Catalogue I. 61.

19. PLUTARCHUS.   Vitae illustrium virorum sive Parallelae.
[c. 147–.]   Large F⁰.

Latin translation edited by J. A. Campanus.
Description in Hain, BM.Catalogue.
Collation in BM.Catalogue.
395 × 287 mm.
Not rubricated, the spaces being still blank.
Binding. Half-pigskin, with wooden boards. Contemporary lettering on
the top edges.
Provenance. On the verso of the flyleaf occurs the inscription, written in
the year 1538 (?), 'Anno D. 38. Leonardus Angermair Capellanus seu
Canonicus Chori Divi Billibaldi [Eichstadt?] dono dedit.' A sale
no. 1646.
HC. *13124.   Proctor 242.   BM.Catalogue I. 62.

HEINRICH EGGESTEIN (1466)

20. CLEMENS V. Constitutiones cum apparatu Joannis Andreae.
[No date.]   Large F⁰.

Description in Hain, BM.Catalogue.
Collation in BM.Catalogue.   But no blank in the first quire, and sig. f
eight leaves only.
394 × 290 mm.   A large crude blue initial, edged with red, on the first leaf.
Ordinary initials and paragraph marks in plain red or blue.   A few
marginal notes (saec. XV).
Binding. Elaborate mosaic, with painted gauffered edges, metal clasps,
knobs and corner pieces (saec. XIX).
Provenance. Not known.
Hain *5413.   Proctor 260.   BM.Catalogue I. 67.

21. ADRIANUS CARTHUSIENSIS.   De remediis utriusque for-
tunae.   [About 1471–2.]   4⁰.

Description in Hain, BM.Catalogue.
Collation in BM.Catalogue.
205 × 140 mm.
Capitals not filled in, initial strokes and underlinings in red.
Binding. Modern red morocco with gold tooling.   Gilt edges.
Provenance. Not recorded.
Hain *94.   Proctor 275.   BM.Catalogue I. 70.

22. BEDA. Historia ecclesiastica gentis Anglorum. [No date.] Fᵒ.

Editio princeps.
Description in Hain, BM.Catalogue.
Collation in BM.Catalogue.
276 × 195 mm.   Initial letters and written headline throughout in plain red ; and rubricated fully, though somewhat carelessly.
Binding. Mottled calf with gilt back and sprinkled edges (eighteenth century).
Provenance. Sir Alexander Boswell † 1822 (with autograph signature and note). Bought of Quaritch, Catalogue 175, no. 24.
Hain *2732.   Proctor 284.   BM.Catalogue I. 71.

PRINTER OF HENRICUS ARIMINENSIS (1476)

23. THOMAS AQUINAS. De veritate catholicae fidei. [No date.] Large Fᵒ.

Description in Hain, BM.Catalogue.
Collation in BM.Catalogue.
400 × 296 mm.   Wants last leaf blank.
Not rubricated.   A few marginal notes (saec. XV).
Binding. Contemporary leather, with diagonal diaper panel and many interesting stamps (rosette, 'Maria,' birds). Metal clasps. (With no. 95.)
Provenance. A Nürnberg duplicate (label removed, see no. 70 A).   Bought from J. and J. Leighton.
Hain *1385.   Proctor 322.   B.M.Catalogue I. 77.   Pellechet 986.

24. THOMAS AQUINAS. Summa secunda secundae partis. [No date.] Large Fᵒ.

Description in Hain, BM.Catalogue.
Collation in BM.Catalogue : but B¹² C¹⁰.
392 × 284 mm.   Not rubricated : but on the first leaf is a large decorative initial letter, crudely executed in red, yellow, and green, with a scroll of the same colours extending round three sides of the page.
Binding. Original oak boards, covered with white skin, stained cherry-colour. The clasps, bosses, and side label have been removed.
Provenance. 'Closter Weihen Stephen 1646' (bookplate), i.e. Weihenstephan in Bavaria.   H. W. Cholmley (1902).
HC. *1455.   Proctor 323   BM.Catalogue I. 79.

HEINRICH KNOBLOCHTZER (1477)

25. ÆSOPUS. Vita et Fabulae. [1481 ?] Small Fº.

Latin translation of Remigius, with his fables, and those of Avianus.
Description and *Collation* in BM.Catalogue, and Morgan Catalogue.
278 × 195 mm. Woodcuts.
Binding. Dark crimson morocco with elaborate blind tooling by Zaehnsdorf.
Provenance. Not known.
BM.Catalogue I. 88.   Proctor 387.   Morgan Catalogue I. 41 (no. 50).
    Schorbach and Spirgatis, no. 37.   Cf. Muther 776–9.   Schreiber 3021.

MARTIN SCHOTT (1485)

26. COLUMNIS (GUIDO DE). Hübsche Hystorie von der königlichen Stadt Troja. 13 March 1489. Small Fº.

Third German edition.
Description in Hain, BM.Catalogue.
Collation in BM.Catalogue.
285 × 203 mm. Three leaves (sig. a 1, i 1, and q 5) are in facsimile. The
    second leaf is damaged. Blank last leaf gone. The second leaf has a
    fine decorative border composed of three strips, the last representing a
    lion hunt. Fine initial letters of three alphabets. Numerous woodcuts,
    some roughly touched with colour.
Binding. Modern brown calf, red edges.
Provenance. No. 323 in some sale.
HC. 5518.   Proctor 401.   BM.Catalogue I. 94–5.   Muther 505.   Schreiber
    4138.

27. AUGUSTINUS. Opus canonum. 1490. Small Fº.

With the commentary of Ambrosius Massarius, edited by Tilmannus
    Limperger.
Description in Hain, BM.Catalogue.
Collation in BM.Catalogue.
282 × 205 mm. Below the colophon and verses by F. D. L. on leaf CXXXIII b,
    is the signature 'Frater Gregorius Darmstatt[ensis].' The two blank
    leaves following are filled with a closely and well written treatise,
    'De devotione,' and the same hand has added a few marginal notes in
    German, to the text.
Initial letters in plain red, and slight rubrication. Woodcuts.

As in the BM. copy the final 'm' of 'mundūm' on the first leaf has been
  covered with a paper label, and the following word 'vivendi' is printed
  upon a label, covering another word.
Binding. Half green cloth with black cloth sides by Carl Wilhelm of
  Stuttgart. Kerr and Richardson of Glasgow (label).
Provenance. 'Frater Gregorius Darmstatt' (saec. XVI). Bookplate of
  Robert Buchanan Stewart (1888).
Hain *2076 (cf. *5683). Proctor 403. BM.Catalogue I. 95. Schreiber 3392.

JOHANN REINHARD OF GRÜNINGEN (1483)

28. TERENTIUS. Comoediae. 1496. Small Fᵒ.

Cum directorio, glosa interlineari, et commentariis Donati, Guidonis, et
  Ascensii.
The first edition with interlinear gloss.
Description in Hain, Schmidt, BM.Catalogue. Fol. 179 b reads 'urbe libera'
  for 'libera urbe' in the colophon.
Collation in BM.Catalogue.
305 × 215 mm. Woodcuts. Rubricated capitals and initial strokes. On folio 1
  of the text a, well-executed initial in puce on green ground has been
  pasted in. Large printed calligraphic initial on the sixth leaf.
At the beginning of the book are inserted four leaves of manuscript of about
  the year 1500. These contain an oration (1487) by Cassandra, 'Dive
  Cassandre fidelis virginis venete in gymnasio Patavino pro Berthuco
  Canonico Concordiensi liberalium artium insignia suscipiente oratio.'
  This is followed by a letter from Ludovicus Scledeus Vincentinus to her,
  and her reply ; and another by Angelus Tancredus Lucanus to her dated
  1488 ; a Sapphic ode by Franciscus Niger in her honour ; a letter by
  Petrus Abietiscola Nerimontanus to her from Nürnberg ; and a Sapphic
  poem by Conrad Celtes to Apollo.
Binding. Original beech boards covered with plain white leather, and
  two metal clasps. Lozenge-shaped large library label at foot of back.
  The end-leaves, pasted down, consist of four leaves of a gradual of the
  fourteenth century.
Provenance. From the Benedictine house at Amorbach : 'Ex Bib mnrij
  Amorb. ord. sti Benedicti.'
HC. *15431. Proctor 473. Schmidt 26. BM.Catalogue I. 110. Morgan
  Catalogue I. 57 (no. 54). Muther 533. Schreiber 5331.

29. HORATIUS. Opera cum annotationibus J. Locher. 12 March
1498. Small Fᵒ.

Description in Hain, BM.Catalogue.

Collation in BM.Catalogue.

301 × 212 mm. Some cuts coloured. For the engraver's initials see fol. LXXXIII.

Binding.   Modern foreign half-leather with paper sides.

Provenance.   The names of two previous owners are on the title; and on the reverse, in a hand of the sixteenth century, the inscription :

> ' Gymnacio
> Magnifici & Generosi D.D. Gregorij Horwath
> aliter Stansith Liberi Baronis &c. domini in
> Graden. & . . . .
> Volumen consecrat F. P.'

Library stamp of the Hungarian Academy of Sciences, with their sale mark as duplicate.

In 1649 the book was in the Jesuit College 'Secpusii.' See the inscription on the title.

HC. *8898. Proctor 485. Schmidt 34. BM.Catalogue I. 112. Muther 535. Schreiber 4240.

JACOBUS EBER (1483)

30. GOBII (JOANNES). Scala coeli. 1483. Small Fº.

Description in BM.Catalogue.

Collation.   Wants [a 1] first leaf.

295 × 207 mm. MS. signatures.

Plain initials, paragraph marks, and red initial strokes. A curious whole page woodcut of the Scala Coeli on a 2*b.*

Binding.   Original oak boards with half leather back. The end-leaves consist of two vellum fragments of an antiphoner of the thirteenth century.

Provenance.   On the title is the inscription : 'Codex monasterij S. Mathiae apostoli' (Trèves?). H. W. Cholmley (1902), lot 727.

Hain 9407. BM.Catalogue I. 118. Figured in Burger, Pl. 25. Schreiber 4368.

BAMBERG

JOHANN SENSENSCHMID WITH HEINRICH PETZENSTEINER (1487)

31. PSALTERIUM LATINUM. [About 1490.] Fº.

Description in Hain, and Morgan Catalogue.

Collation in Morgan Catalogue.

265 × 202 mm.   Plainly rubricated.

Binding. Half binding of white pigskin (with tooling), and wooden boards with clasps (saec. XVI).

Provenance. The name of 'S. Elysabett Portzlerin' written on the inside of the front cover.

Bookplate, 'Ex libris M. L. R. de Samareio. Bibliothèques de Semallé et de la Gastine.'

Hain *13466. Morgan I. 70 (no. 73).

COLOGNE

ULRICH ZEL (1466)

32. AUGUSTINUS.   De vita christiana et de singularitate clericorum.   1467.   Small 4°.

Description in Hain, BM., and Morgan Catalogues.
Collation in BM. Catalogue, and Morgan Catalogue (imperfect).
210 × 138 mm.
This volume consists of two tracts, considered by Proctor as one book :
  (1) De vita christiana [Hain *2094], and (2) De singularitate clericorum [Hain *2082]. At the head of the first leaf is written in bold style the inscription : 'Ad Sororem' (modern).
Only slight rubrication.   First leaf (blank) gone.
Binding. Brown morocco with blind lace-tool bordering, by J. Faulkner, London.
Provenance. Inglis (1900) no. 64.
Hain *2094, *2082 (Copinger).   Proctor 802.   Voulliéme 201.   BM. Catalogue I. 180.   Morgan I. 73 (no. 75).

33. PIUS II.   Epistola ad Mahumetem.   [No date.]   Small 4°.

Description and *Collation* in BM. Catalogue.
215 × 140 mm.   With the first leaf containing the fragment of Virgil's Eclogues ('Qui te pollio,' etc.), on the presence of which in this book Mr F. Jenkinson speaks in his Sandars Lecture of 1909 :
'The text begins on the second leaf, but the first leaf, instead of being blank, contains a page from Zell's edition of Virgil's *Eclogues*. This page is the recto of the seventh leaf of the book ; and it is clear that that ought to have been printed on a half sheet which had already had one or both sides of the second leaf printed on it. An impression of it on a half sheet of which the other three pages were blank was *ipso facto*

waste. The printing of the *Epistola* must either have been going on at the time or have been begun very soon afterwards. The first leaf was to be a blank. It and leaf 8 would be printed on one half sheet. Either from inadvertence or more probably to economize paper, instead of a clean half sheet, the printer used the one which on one of the pages not wanted for the *Epistola* already contained the page of *Eclogues*. And from this we may infer that the blank leaf at the beginning of a book is at any rate in some cases not so much a rudimentary title-page as an expedient for keeping the first page of the book clean, in fact a wrapper. The removal of this leaf when the book came to be bound may have been intended.'

Rubricated. The first initial letter parti-coloured in blue and red.
Binding. Smooth dark brown morocco, with blind tooling, by Hayday.
Provenance. B. Quaritch, 1902.
HC. *171. Proctor 816. BM. Catalogue I. 182. Voulliéme 960.

34. GERSON (JOHANNES). De cognitione castitatis et pollutionibus diurnis. [No date.] Small 4º.

Description and *Collation* in BM.Catalogue.
206 × 136 mm.
Plain rubrication. A few marginal notes.
Binding. See no. 37.
Provenance. Ibid.
Hain *7692. Proctor 831. BM.Catalogue I. 184. Voulliéme 488.

35. GERSON (JOHANNES). De custodia linguæ. [No date.] Small 4º.

Description and *Collation* in BM.Catalogue.
206 × 136 mm.
Plain rubrication. Some marginal notes.
Binding. See no. 37.
Provenance. Ibid.
Hain *7683. Proctor 834. BM. Catalogue I. 184. Voulliéme 470.

36. GERSON (JOHANNES). De efficacia orationis, etc. [No date.] 4º.

Description in Hain, BM.Catalogue.
Collation in BM.
206 × 136 mm. Capitals, paragraph marks and init al strokes in red.
This copy begins 'It,' not 'it' (cf. Hain).

Binding. See no. 37.
Provenance. Ibid.
Hain *7687.   Proctor 835.   BM.Catalogue I. 184.   Voulliéme 475.

37. GERSON (JOHANNES).   De pollutionibus nocturnis. [No
date.]   4°.

Description in Hain, BM.Catalogue.
Collation in BM.Catalogue.
206 × 136 mm.   Capitals, paragraph-marks, and initial strokes in red.
A few marginal notes.
The first of a volume of tracts printed for the most part at Cologne.   The
   others bound with it are nos. 34, 35, 36, 40, 56, 59, 64, and 176.
Binding.   Crimson morocco with gold tooling, by C. Smith.
Provenance.   The collection was made at an early date, for there is a table
   of contents written at the beginning in handwriting of about the year
   1500, with the library class mark : A 6, and at foot the initials : F ST G.
   On the first leaf at foot is the inscription in seventeenth century hand :
   'Conventus Tremon*ensis* Ord*inis* Fra*tr*um Praed*icatorum*' (Dortmund).
Hain *7696.   Proctor 837.   BM.Catalogue I. 184.   Voulliéme 478.

38. PIUS II.   De duobus amantibus.   [No date.]   4°.

Description in Hain, and Voulliéme.
Collation [a–d⁸ e⁶].
205 × 142 mm.   Not rubricated.
Binding.   Old red morocco with gilt tooling and edges.   With part of
   leaf CCXLV of the Nürnberg Chronicle of 1493, containing the story,
   inserted at end.
Provenance.   Inglis (1871), no. 138.   Boone.   W. H. Crawford, bookplate
   (1891).   Quaritch.
Hain *213.   Voulliéme 942.

39. RODERICUS ZAMORENSIS.   Speculum vitæ humanae.
[1472.]   4°.

Description in BM. Catalogue, Hain (203 leaves only).
Collation in BM. Catalogue.
196 × 136 mm.   The first edition.   Plain rubrication, carelessly applied.
   Two blank leaves at end gone.
Binding.   Chocolate calf, with gilt tooling and red edges.
Provenance.   On the first leaf is the library stamp, 'Dem Kloster Raggen-
   burg.'   Edward Shipperdson (1887) with bookplate.
Hain *13933.   Proctor 852.   BM. Catalogue I. 187.   Voulliéme 1025.

40. AUGUSTINUS. De fuga mulierum, de continentia, de contemptu mundi, Hieronymi epistola ad Paulinum presbyterum, Augustini sermo de communi vita clericorum. [Ab. 1470.] 4º.

Description in Voulliéme.
Collation [a–c⁸].
206 × 136 mm.
Binding. See no. 37.
Provenance. Ibid.
Voulliéme 212. Cf. HC. 1962. Proctor 861.

41. AUGUSTINUS. Epistola ad Cyrillum de magnificentiis Hieronymi, etc. [No date.] 4º.

Description in BM.Catalogue, Hain (see note below).
Collation in BM.Catalogue.
210 × 146 mm. Leaves 1–16 only. Rubricated.
Binding. Old green morocco, gilt edges (with no. 42).
Provenance. J. and J. Leighton Catalogue (1905, no. 294).
HC. *6719 (2). Proctor 862. BM. Catalogue I. 188. Voulliéme· 187.
     Morgan I. 76–7 (84).

Hain-Copinger *6719 (corrected).
1–47. Eusebius.
48–56. Epistola Augustini ad Cyrillum de magnificentiis Ieronymi.
57–98. Epistola Cyrilli.

41 A. —— [Another copy.]

212 × 147 mm. Wants leaves 1–9. Rubricated.
This, though imperfect, makes with no. 41 a complete copy.
Binding. Modern plain brown morocco.
Provenance. J. and J. Leighton.
See last entry.

42. EUSEBIUS. Epistola de morte Hieronymi. [No date.] 4º.
Description in BM.Catalogue, Hain.
Collation in BM.Catalogue.
210 × 146 mm. Rubricated. Wants leaves 1–16.
Binding and *Provenance.* With no. 41.
HC. *6719 (1). BM.Catalogue I. 189. Voulliéme 403. Proctor 862.

43. CARACCIOLUS (ROBERTUS) DE LICIO.   Sermones quadragesimales.   17 January 1473.   Small Fᵒ.

Description in Hain, BM.Catalogue.
Collation in BM. Catalogue.   This copy wants first leaf (blank) and last leaf.
293 × 215 mm.   Rubricated with plain red initials, two with attempted
   illumination, in brown ink.   Initial directors.   A few marginal notes.
   One leaf of contemporary medical matter in Latin and German ; and
   three leaves of Latin ascetical notes on the preliminary fly-leaves.
Binding.   Contemporary brown leather, with lozenge diaper panel, and
   numerous stamps, in fine preservation.
Provenance.   Formerly in the Jesuit College at Munster.   At the foot of the
   first and last page the inscription :
          'Liber Collegij Societatis Jesu Monasterij.'
   The name of the original donor of the volume is commemorated in writing
   on the inside of the front cover :
          'Hunc librum legavit Dominus Petrus de Dusseldorp......?'
   The book had formerly two clasps and has been chained.
Bought of Ellis in 1903.
Hain *4429.   Proctor 880.   BM.Catalogue I. 191–2.   Voulliéme 307.

44. LEONARDUS DE UTINO.   Sermones de Sanctis.   1473.
Small Fᵒ.

Description in Voulliéme.
Collation as in BM.Catalogue (no leaf 210 inserted, y 8 cut away, CC 8
   gone).
300 × 214 mm.   2 vols.   Before rubrication.   Initial strokes.
Binding.   Original leather, with diagonal tooling ; clasps gone.   One vellum
   label remaining (on second volume).
Provenance.   At the end of the first volume is the note :
'Hos sermones cum alio volumine soluit apud Valencianas spectabilis
   dominus utriusque juris doctor dominus Guillelmus Goneti petente ab
   eo elemoᵃ fratre petro de chassoᵗᵒ....anno 1477.   Orate pro eo Nam ita
   est.   Pe Chassoᵗᵒ....'
Signature of Lt. Col. C. E. Watson, 1867.   Quaritch, 1902.
Hain *16128.   Proctor 881.   Voulliéme 741.   Cf. BM.Catalogue I. 192.

45. AEGIDIUS DE ASSISIO.   Aurea verba de gratia Dei, virtutibus et vitiis.   [No date.]   4ᵒ.

Description in Hain, BM.Catalogue.
Collation in BM.Catalogue.
211 × 145 mm.   Rubricated roughly.

S. C.

Binding.   Modern black morocco.
Provenance.   On the verso of the last leaf is the contemporary inscription :
Dominus Walterus pastor quondam ecclesie in osporē librum hunc contulit
   monasterio sancti Maximini extra muros treverenses sito, etc. etc.
No. 2792 in some auction.
HC. *105.   Proctor 884.   BM.Catalogue I. 193.   Voulliéme 7.

46.   BONAVENTURA.   Regimen conscientiae, &c.   [No date.]   4º.

Description in Hain, BM.Catalogue.
Collation in BM.Catalogue.   This copy contains leaves 1–19 only, the first
   tract.
208 × 140 mm.   Rubrication plain.
Binding.   Modern brown calf by I. Petit.
Provenance.   J. and J. Leighton.
HC. *3498.   BM.Catalogue I. 193.   Voulliéme 275.

47.   EUSEBIUS.   Evangelica Praeparatio.   [No date.]   Fº.

Ed. 1 of the translation by G. Trapezuntius.
Description in BM.Catalogue.
Collation, ibid.   Sig. m has 10 leaves only.
290 × 217 mm.   The initials in plain red, only the first thirteen leaves
   slightly rubricated.
Binding.   Modern crimson morocco.
Provenance.   W. H. Crawford (1891) with bookplate.
Hain 6698.   Proctor 891.   BM.Catalogue I. 194.   Voulliéme 402.

48.   NIDER (JOHANNES).   Praeceptorium.   [No date.]   Small Fº.

Description in BM.Catalogue.
Collation, ibid.   Last leaf, blank, gone.
283 × 205 mm.   Rubricated, with plain red initials, throughout.   The first
   initial on the first page painted in blue and red.
Binding.   Plain brown calf (eighteenth century) with some blind tooling.
Provenance.   Duplicate stamp of the Lubeck Town Library and the auto-
   graph signature of 'W. G. Thorpe' on the first leaf.   J. and J. Leighton.
Hain *11780.   Proctor 899.   BM. Catalogue I. 194 (second entry).
   Voulliéme 856.

49.   NIDER (JOHANNES).   Praeceptorium.   [No date.]   Small Fº.

Description in BM.Catalogue ; cf. Voulliéme.
Collation, ibid.   Last leaf, blank, gone.

293 × 212 mm. Rubricated, with red initials slightly elaborated, throughout. A few decorative line-endings in the prefatory index. A contemporary manuscript foliation and signature occur at the foot of the leaf, nearly throughout.

The headline of 'Preceptum primum capitulum septimum' has been misprinted 'undecimum' and corrected contemporaneously by pen. The printed headlines cease after Preceptum primum capitulum duodecimum.

Binding. Contemporary brown leather with diaper panel pattern: two stamps (1) quatrefoil, (2) lamb with pennon. Formerly with two clasps. Rebacked.

Provenance. H. W. Cholmley (1902), No. 774.

BM.Catalogue I. 194 (first entry). Cf. Voulliéme 857. Proctor 900.

50. RODERICUS ZAMORENSIS. Epistola lugubris de expugnatione Euboiae. [No date.] Small Fᵒ.

Description in Hain, BM.Catalogue.
Collation, BM.Catalogue.
275 × 19 mm. Capitals and paragraph marks in red. Initial strokes in red or yellow. MS. note, qu. by Askew?, inserted.
Binding with No. 2.
Provenance, ibid.
Hain 13956 = *13957. Proctor 900* [additions. Vol. II. p. 903]. BM. Catalogue I. 165. Voulliéme 1024.

51. JACOBUS DE VORAGINE. Legenda Aurea. 1483. Small Fᵒ.

Description in BM.Catalogue.
Collation, ibid.
286 × 210 mm. Rubricated with plain red initial letters. On the first leaf of the text, following the table, are two elaborate initials, 'U' red and brown, 'A' blue, red and gold. Badly stained at end.

Binding. Contemporary brown leather on wooden boards. Diaper panel. Stamps: rosette, fleur-de-lis, lozenge, mullet, lamb and pennon. Rebacked in the sixteenth century with roll LUCRE(tia), IUSTIC(ia), PRUDE(ntia), 1558. Original metal clasps.

Provenance. Charles Leeson Prince, with his bookplate 1882; note by him inside the front cover, and a note by Mr F. Jenkinson inserted.

At the head of the second leaf is a manuscript note of former ownership (seventeenth century): 'Bibliotheca man in...' (erased).

BM.Catalogue I. 197. Proctor 905. Copinger 6434. Voulliéme 623.

52. KEYERSLACH (PETRUS).   Passio Christi cum quattuor evangelistis, etc.   ' 1487 '.   [About 1495.]   Small 4º.

Editio princeps.
Description in Hain.
Collation, a–d⁸ e¹⁰.
205 × 137 mm.
42 leaves. With woodcut of the crucifixion on the first page and repeated at sig. d 2 *b*. Rubricated.
Binding. Paper wrapper.
Provenance. J. and J. Leighton.
Hain *9779. Proctor †908. Voulliéme 717. Schreiber 4458.

53. GULIELMUS DE GOUDA.   Tractatus de expositione missae. [No date.] Small 4º.

Description in Hain, BM.Catalogue.
Collation in BM.Catalogue.   First leaf and last leaf (blank) gone.
202 × 135 mm.   Not rubricated.
Binding. Modern crimson morocco.
Provenance. Leighton.
Hain *7825. Proctor 916. BM.Catalogue I. 199. Voulliéme 522.

54. THOMAS DE AQUINO.   De corpore Christi.   Acc. N. de Lyra de sacramento et alicujus super oratione dominica. [Ab. 1485.] Small 4º.

Description in Voulliéme.
Collation, ab⁸ c⁶.
205 × 137 mm.   Rubricated with plain red or blue initials and paragraph marks.   The first initial more ornate, blue with red feathering.
Binding. Modern cream-colour paper with stiff boards.
Provenance. No. 35743 in Rosenthal's stock.
Voulliéme 1165. Copinger 544. Pellechet 978. Ennen 132.

ARNOLD TER HOERNEN (1470)

55. BURLEY (WALTER).   De vita et moribus philosophorum. 1472. Small 4º.

Description in HC.
Collation [a–l⁸ m¹⁰]. Misbound.

203 × 137 mm.
The first dated edition of this book, written about 1337. Plainly rubricated.
Binding. Common half-calf with paper sides (about 1800).
Provenance. W. Morris (1898, book label), no. 102.
HC. 4122. Proctor †931. Voulliéme 295. Morgan I. 75 (no. 81).

56. ROLEVINCK (WERNER). Tractatulus de forma visitationum monasticarum. [Ab. 1475.] Small 4⁰.

Description in Voulliéme.
Collation, a⁸ b⁶.
206 × 138 mm. Plain rubrication.
Binding. Bound with no. 37.
Provenance. Ibid.
Voulliéme 1054. Copinger iii. 5858. Campbell 1676.

57. FLORUS. Epitoma de cursu et statu Romanorum. Acc. [Jordani] de commendatione romani imperii. [Ab. 1474.] Small F⁰.

Description in HC., BM.Catalogue, Voulliéme.
Collation, BM.Catalogue.
282 × 213 mm. Not rubricated. Contemporary marginal notes. Originally part of a volume of which it formed ff. 175–203.
Binding. Plain red morocco by Duru 1853, with gilt edges.
Provenance. Firmin Didot (book label).
HC. 7199. Proctor 974. BM.Catalogue I. 202–3. Voulliéme 419.

PRINTER OF 'DICTYS'

58. SALLUSTIUS. Invectiva contra M. T. Ciceronem, etc. [Ab. 1470.] Small 4⁰.

Description. 1 *a.* A. G. Salustio invectiua cōtra . M. T. Ciceronem
   2 *b.* Responsio . M. T. Ciceronis contra in|uectiuā . G. Salustij
   4 *b.* Incipit eplā egregia enee siluij poete cōtra vernan|dum legisperitū
   de recōmendacione poesis : 8 *b.* Leonardi Arentini (*sic*) Epitaphium
   ab | Enea siluio . senēn poeta editum.
As this book bears a close relationship to nos. 60 and 61, they may be
   described together. Though now bound separately, they have obviously
   been bound together from a very early period. They are not rubricated,

but the initial letters and marginal illustrations are most exquisitely drawn in pen and brown ink, representing grotesques. It is difficult to speak too highly of the artist's work. Unfortunately here and there the binder has worked his usual havoc in the margin. On the first leaf besides an initial dragon G are at foot three separate figures, one playing the tabor, the second blowing a horn. These two are male figures and are clad in grotesque drapery. The third figure is that of a female playing a lute, her body displayed, but her robe and long hair flowing behind. On the second leaf is an angel forming part of an initial A. On the fourth leaf sprays of oak and thistle. The decoration of the companion volumes is described under their own numbers (60 and 61).

Collation [ab⁴].

195 × 134 mm.

Binding. Whole red morocco by Rivière and Son.

Provenance. Not recorded.

Hain 14236 (no other copy recorded). Cf. Voulliéme, p. 417 (s.v. Pius II).

PRINTER OF 'DARES' (AFTER 14 APRIL 1470)

59. HIERONYMUS. Ordo vivendi Deo. [Ab. 1472.] Small 4º.

Description in Voulliéme, HC.

Collation [a–c⁸ d⁶].

206 × 137 mm. Plain rubrication.

Binding. Bound with no. 37.

Provenance. Ibid.

Voulliéme 577. HC. *8569.

60. SENECA. De remediis fortuitorum. [Ab. 1472.] Small 4º.

Description in Hain, BM.Catalogue.

Collation, BM.Catalogue.

195 × 136 mm.

Possibly the first edition. Not rubricated. For the decoration in brown ink see the note on no. 58. In this tract this consists of an initial H, and the figures of an armed knight standing, holding a lance with pennon of a star and crescent, and a youthful figure seated at his feet with hands crossed on breast. These form the letter L.

Binding. Plain red polished morocco by Rivière and Son. Originally bound with nos. 58 and 61.

Provenance. Not recorded.

Hain *14655. Proctor 999. BM.Catalogue I. 213. Voulliéme 1070.

PRINTER OF 'HISTORIA SANCTI ALBANI'

61. SENECA. De quattuor virtutibus, etc. [No date.] Small 4º.

Description in BM.Catalogue, Voulliéme.
Collation, BM.Catalogue. See H. Bradshaw, *Collected Papers*, p. 154.
196 × 135 mm.
Possibly the first edition. Exquisitely decorated with marginal drawings in brown ink by the same artist as nos. 58 and 60. The initial Q on the first page represents the Annunciation angel and the Blessed Virgin. In the scroll uniting their heads are the initials 'A. G. P. D. T. M.' (Ave, Gratia Plena, Dominus Tecum Maria). On sig. 6 *b* the initial O represents two lions in circle with tails knotted. 10 *b* and 11 *a* and *b*, floral work. 13 *b* initial G of bird and figure blowing a horn. Some marginal contemporary notes on 17 *b* and 19 *b*.
Binding. Polished red morocco by Rivière and Son as no. 58.
Provenance. Not recorded.
BM. Catalogue I. 214. Proctor 1003. Bradshaw 2. Voulliéme 1072.

JOHANN KOELHOFF, THE ELDER (1472)

62. BONAVENTURA. Diaeta salutis. 1474. Small F^o.

Description in BM.Catalogue, Voulliéme.
Collation in BM.Catalogue.
288 × 210 mm. Rubricated, with plain initials.
Binding. Original wooden boards covered with brown leather and diaper panel.
Stamps : IHESUS, eagle, rosette fleur de lis.
Bound with no. 66.
Provenance. On the verso of a vellum flyleaf in this book is the following inscription :
'Hunc librum et multos alios bonos libros donavit nobis venerabilis dominus Hermannus de Langhen decanus ecclesie Mon[acensis?] singularissimus fautor sustentator et promotor noster pro quo merito fideliter orare debemus cum et multa bona nobis fecit ut plenius in libro benefactorum videri poterit.'
Old library class mark G. 35 (altered to 37).
HC. 3528. BM.Catalogue I. 219. Voulliéme 273.

PRINTER OF FLORES SANCTI AUGUSTINI (1473)

63. BURLEY (WALTER). De vita et moribus philosophorum. [1472?] Small F⁰.

Description in Hain, Voulliéme, BM.Catalogue.
Collation in BM.Catalogue.
290 × 200 mm.
Rubricated, plain red initials, the first left blank for more elaborate decoration.
Binding. Red morocco with gilt back, and arms of Philip V on the sides.
Provenance. Copy bound for Philip V of Spain (†1746). Sold by Payne and Foss. Syston Park (1884, both bookplates). J. and J. Leighton.
Hain *4113. Proctor 1106. BM.Catalogue I. 234. Voulliéme 296.

NICHOLAS GOTZ

64. DISPUTATIO inter clericum et militem. Compendium de vita antichristi. [Ab. 1475.] Small 4⁰.

Description in Voulliéme.
Collation [ab⁸].
206 × 136 mm. Plain rubrication.
Binding. Bound with no. 37.
Provenance. Ibid.
Voulliéme 378. Copinger III. 1963 a.

CONRAD WINTERS, OF HOMBURG (1476–1482)

65. PETRUS COMESTOR. Historia Scholastica. [Before 20 September 1479?] Small F⁰.

Description in Hain, Voulliéme, BM.Catalogue.
Collation in BM. Catalogue. Sig. [H] is supplied in contemporary MS.
285 × 206 mm. Not rubricated.
Some early Latin Verses (ab. 1500) on Petrus Comestor at the beginning, and others at end. On the second fly-leaf 'Solus Deus Protector meus W[estmorland]' (seventeenth century).
Binding. Original wooden boards bevelled. Ornate diaper panel surrounded with the scroll 'IHS · MARIA.'
Provenance. Arthur Darcy (saec. XVI, with signature). Earl of Westmorland ('1856').
HC. *5530. Proctor 1176. BM.Catalogue I. 247. Voulliéme 915.

66. HIERONYMUS. Vitas sanctorum patrum. [Before 20 September 1479.] F°.

Description in Voulliéme.
Collation as in BM.Catalogue.   Wants [a 1 and n 6] both blank, cut away.
288×212 mm.   Plain rubrication.
Binding.   Bound with no. 62.
Provenance.   Ibid.
Hain 8586.   Voulliéme 1252.   Proctor 1182.   BM.Catalogue I. 246–7.
 Copinger III. 2959.

67. GERARDUS DE VLIEDERHOVEN.   Cordiale quattuor novissimorum.   [Between 17 March and 20 September 1479.]   4°.

Description in BM.Catalogue.
Collation, ibid.   Last leaf, blank, gone.
203×140 mm.   Capitals and paragraph marks in blue.   Initial strokes
 in red.
Binding.   Common modern vellum.
Provenance.   ? Rosenthal of Munich.
Hain *5699.   Proctor 1187.   BM.Catalogue I. 246.   Voulliéme 450.

JOHANN GULDENSCHAFF (1477)

68. ALBERTUS MAGNUS.   Legenda Alberti Magni.   [Before
1484.]   Small 4°.

By Petrus de Prussia or Rudolphus de Noviomago.
Description in BM.Catalogue, Voulliéme.
Collation in BM.Catalogue.
201 × 133 mm.
Capitals, paragraph-marks, initial-strokes in red.
The date ' Mcccc° lxxxiij°.   3° ydus Januarij ' occurs on sig. f i.
Some marginal notes (saec. XVII).
Binding.   Bound in half-vellum (saec. XIX).
Provenance. . ? Rosenthal.
Not in Hain (cf. 11915).   Proctor 1209.   Voulliéme 936.   BM. Catalogue
 I. 255.

69. PHARETRA, auctoritates et dicta doctorum philosophorum et poetarum continens. [Ab. 1478.] Large F⁰.

Description in Hain, Voulliéme.

Collation [*⁶ a–c¹⁰ d⁸ e–k¹⁰ l⁸ m¹⁰ n⁸ o¹⁰ p⁸ q⁶ r⁸ s–z, aa–dd¹⁰ ee⁸ ff¹⁰ gg⁸ hh⁸ ii–ll¹⁰]. Wants first leaf blank.

383×286 mm. One initial letter parti-coloured in blue and red. Plain smaller initials and paragraph marks in blue or red.

Binding. Original brown leather over beech boards, with diaper panel, and stamps, a stag, and 'Maria hilf.' Remains of metal clasps, with legend 'Ave' 'Maria' 'uns.' Lower cover partly stripped.

Provenance. The fly-leaf contains the inscription 'Io. 216. Antonj Annenberger,' about 1500. Canon J. E. Millard (1895), bookplate.

Panzer IV. 176, 954. Hain *12907. Voulliéme 938.

AUGSBURG

GÜNTHER ZAINER (1468)

70. RODERICUS ZAMORENSIS.   Speculum vitae humanae. 11 Jan. 1471. Small F⁰.

Description in Hain and BM.Catalogue.

Collation in BM.Catalogue [a–m¹⁰ n⁸]. 128 leaves.

286 × 192 mm. Rubricated. Initial letter in red and blue with grotesques. Note that the last line on fol. 58 *b* was printed later, to supply an omission.

Binding. Green morocco, with back tooled in gold.

Provenance. Sold by Longman in 1825. Syston Párk (1884, with both bookplates).

70 A. —— Another copy.

300 × 212 mm. Plain red initial letters ; the first, ornate red and blue.

Binding. Olive morocco with elaborate blind tooling.

Provenance. Duplicate from the Nürnberg Library, with library bookplate pasted upon the first initial. Sold in London in 1821 for 5 guineas. Again by Ellis in Jan. 1866. H. W. Cholmley (1902, with bookplate).

For third copy see Appendix.

Hain-Copinger *13940. Proctor 1525. BM.Catalogue II. 316.

71. AEGIDIUS ROMANUS. De regimine principum. 1473.
Large F°.

Description in Hain and BM.Catalogue.
Collation [**⁴ a⁸ b–g¹⁰ h⁸ ik¹⁰ l⁸⁺¹ mn¹⁰]. 129 leaves.
395 × 283 mm.   Plain rubrication over woodcut initials.
Binding.   Red morocco by Rivière and Son.   Gilt edges.
Provenance.   Not recorded.
Hain *107.   Proctor 1535.   BM.Catalogue II. 319.

72. JACOBUS DE VORAGINE. Legenda aurea. [Ab. 1474.]
Small F°.

Description [1 *b*. Incipit plogus sup legendas santo2+ *gone.*] 3*a*. Incipit
plogus sup legenda scto2+ quā spila-|uit fr̄ iacob⁹ natōe | anuēf ordīs
fr̄m p̄dicato2+.   400*a*. Hystoria lombardica sancto2+ finit feliciter.
Morgan Catalogue.
Collation [A², a–z, aa–qq¹⁰, rr⁸].   Wants first two leaves, and numbered
leaves 22, 39, 51, 94, 103, 113, 136, 150, 163, 222, 233, 239, 258, 279,
284, 301, 305, 317, 325–6, 331, 348, 354, 361 = 26 leaves.
284 × 210 mm.
The first illustrated edition of this book.   In this imperfect copy, there are
138 woodcuts, representing saints, with contemporary colouring.
Latin.   'Maiblumen' initials, also coloured slightly, with plain paragraph
printed initials filled with colour.   Initial strokes red.   A few con-
temporary marginal notes.
For a note on this book by William Morris see Morgan Catalogue.
Binding.   Brown calf about 1850.
Provenance.   No. 1389 in some sale.
Proctor 1559.   Morgan I. 118 (no. 134).   Copinger III. 6387 (incorrect).
Schreiber 4326.

MONASTERY OF SS. ULRICH AND AFRA

73. SPECULUM HUMANAE SALVATIONIS. [Not after 1473.]
Small F°.

In Latin and German.   The only Latin edition printed with movable type
(Gunther Zainer's type).   It is succeeded by the Seven Joys of the
Blessed Virgin.
Description in Hain (wanting first leaf blank) and BM.Catalogue.
Collation in BM.Catalogue [*, a–z, & 9 *4*¹⁰].   270 leaves.
292 × 210 mm.

Capitals and paragraph marks in plain red and blue. Initial strokes red.
176 cuts, making 192 by repetition. Contemporary colouring in the
woodcuts, four of which illustrate each chapter of the book. A few
contemporary marginal annotations.

Binding. Modern brown morocco with gilt tooling, and the arms in centre
with legend 'Musgrave de Edenhall' (Bart., Co. Cumberland).

Provenance. 'G. Musgrave 1842' on the fly-leaf. Quaritch, 9 Dec. 1901.

Hain *14929. Proctor 1542 (=1631). Bibl. Spencer IV. 9. BM.Catalogue
II. 338–9. Schreiber 5273.

JOHANN SCHÜSSLER (1470)

74. PETRUS DE CRESCENTIIS. Liber ruralium commodorum.
1471. Small F°.

Editio princeps.

Description in Hain.

Collation [a–s^{10} + 10✳ quod pars t^{10} + 10✳ vulpes v^{10} + 10✳ viridarius, x^8]. 211
leaves.

300 × 216 mm. Title initial in green and red, the rest in plain red.

Binding. Original boards covered with white skin and tooled. Rebacked
with vellum.

Provenance. This copy belonged to the Cistercian house of Our Lady in
Furstenfeld in the diocese of Freising, to which it was given in 1472:
"Liber Scte Marie in Campoprincipum Cysterciensis Ordinis Frysingensis
dyocesis. Comparatus per Reverendum patrem Dominum Judocum...
anno domini 1472."

At the foot of the first leaf is the inscription in red ink:
          "Liber sancte marie Infrafurstenfeld."

On the last leaf is the further inscription:
          "Liber sancte Marie Virginis
          Infurstenfeld. 1472."

Apparently a Munich Library duplicate.

Hain-Copinger *5828. Proctor 1590. BM.Catalogue II. 328.

75. AMBROSIUS. Hexameron. 1472. Small F°.

Description in Hain, BM.Catalogue.

Collation [ab^{10} + 10✳ et humidus, c^{10} d^{8+1} e^8 fg^{10} h^8]. 77 leaves. Last leaf
gone.

312 × 215 mm.

Principal initials of the 'maiblumen' type, apparently by the same hand as
no. 76 (qu. same volume?). Ordinary initials in plain red. A few
marginal notes in an Italian hand (saec. XV).

Binding. Modern morocco by Leighton.
Provenance. With no. 76.
Hain *903. Proctor 1595. BM. II. 329.

76. TURRECREMATA (JOHANNES DE). Expositio Psalterii. 1472. Small Fᵒ.

Description in Hain, BM.Catalogue.
Collation [a¹² bc¹⁰ d⁸⁺¹ e–n¹⁰ o⁴]. 135 leaves. Leaves 1 and 134–5 blank. 312×215 mm.
Principal initials 'maiblumen' type from the same hand as no. 75. Ordinary ones in plain red. Marginal notes (saec. XVI).
Binding. Modern brown morocco, by Leighton.
Provenance. 'Monachii ad PP. Franciscanos pro bibl.' J. and J. Leighton (originally with no. 75).
Hain *15696. Proctor 1596. BM.Catalogue II. 329.

77. THERAMO (JACOBUS DE). Consolatio peccatorum sive Belial. 2 July 1472. Small Fᵒ.

The second edition with a date. Dedicated to Pope Urban VI.
Description in BM.Catalogue and Morgan Catalogue.
Collation, ibid.
300×210 mm.
Initial letters in plain blue or red. Initial strokes red, and biblical references underlined in red. Initial directors.
Binding. Red morocco (eighteenth century).
Provenance. Belonged in the fifteenth century to some conventual house at Frankfurt but the name (on the first leaf) has been erased. Early class-mark 'R. 16.'
Wodhull (1886) no. 2556: bought by him at 'Card.. Lomenie's auction' in 1792. ('M. Wodhull July 16th 1792.')
Proctor 1597. Morgan I. 107 (no. 126). BM.Catalogue II. 329.

JOHANN BÄMLER (1472–1493)

78. JOHANNES FRIBURGENSIS. Summa Confessionum. 1472. Small Fᵒ.

German.
Description in Hain and BM. Catalogue.
Collation [*, **, a–e⁸ f¹⁰ g⁴ h¹² i⁶ k¹⁰ l–z, A–G⁸ H⁴ I¹⁰]. Last two (blank?) gone. 272 leaves. (Hain, 276 leaves.)

310 × 212 mm.

The first leaf of the text contains a fairly executed floral border extending
round three sides of the margin, with a large initial letter on burnished
gold ground.   Ordinary initials in plain red, blue or green.   Some
rubrication, and initial strokes in red.

Binding. Modern vellum. Gilt edges.

Provenance. Royal Society of London (originally the gift to them of
Henry Howard, sixth duke of Norfolk, in 1667).

Hain *7367.   Proctor 1599.   BM.Catalogue II. 331.

79. LEHRE und Unterweisung, wie ein Junger Mensch sich
erhalten soll. 1472. Small F°.

Description in Hain and BM.Catalogue.

Fragment only, fol. 51–60.

251 × 178 mm.

The fragment contains: 'Diss ist ain epistel Francisci Petrarche Von grosser
stätikeyt ainer frawen Grÿsel gehaissen.'   The second German issue
of this story.

The first initial (qu. modern?) deep blue with blue and red ornamentation.
Ordinary initials in plain red.

Binding.   Red morocco by Chambolle-Duru, with the Seillière arms on the
sides.

Provenance.   Baron Seillière (1887).

Panzer, *Annalen* I. 69.   Hain *10005.   Proctor 1602.   Cf. BM. II. 331
(wanting this part).

ANTON SORG (1475)

80. AUGUSTINUS.   Liber qui vocatur Quinquaginta.   1475.
Small F°.

Description in Hain and BM.Catalogue.

Collation [a¹⁰ b¹⁰⁺¹ c⁸ d¹² ef¹⁰ g⁶ h¹⁰ i¹²⁺¹].   92 leaves.

285 × 205 mm.   Large and smaller initials in plain red.   Printed initial
directors.   A few marginal notes.

Binding.   Brown calf with simple gilt tooling by Hawes in 1867.

Provenance.   Bought from F. S. Ellis in January 1866.

Hain *1987.   Proctor 1641.   BM.Catalogue II. 341.

81. CATO.   Disticha.   2 November 1475.   Small F°.

Known also as 'Cato Moralizatus.'   The Speculum regiminis of Philippus
de Bergamo.

Description in Hain and BM.Catalogue.

Collation [a–e¹⁰ f⁶, a–z, aa–tt¹⁰ vv⁸].   484 leaves.   (Hain gives 486 leaves.)
This copy reads 'festi' in the eighth line of the colophon.
297 × 208 mm.   Plain initials in red or blue throughout, and initial strokes
    red.   A large written headline in red ink on every page of the book.
Binding.   Blue morocco with plain gold border by C. Smith (XIX cent.).
Provenance.   Syston Park (1884) and Henry White (1902) with both book-
    plates.
Hain *4711.   Proctor 1643.   BM.Catalogue II. 342.

82.   AMBROSIUS.   Expositio in Evangelium Lucae.   1476.
Small Fᵒ.

Description in Hain and BM.Catalogue.
Collation [ab¹⁰ c¹² e–n¹⁰ and 8 op¹⁰ q⁶⁺¹ r¹⁰].   159 leaves.
286 × 204 mm.   The ten printed capitals delicately hand-coloured in pink
    and ochre.   The smaller capitals filled in with red.
Binding.   Red morocco with gold lines (XIX cent.).
Provenance.   A mark of former ownership on the first leaf has been erased.
    Syston Park (1884) and Henry White (1902), with bookplates.
Hain *900.   Proctor 1648.   BM.Catalogue II. 344.

AMBROS KELLER (1479)

83.   ARISTOTELES.   Elenchi, topica.   21 October 1479.   Small Fᵒ.

Latin, Part III of a selection of the Works, translated by Johannes
    Argyropulus.
Description in Hain and BM.Catalogue.
Collation [a–c (gone) d–i¹⁰ k⁸ l¹⁰].   104 leaves.   Leaves 1–26 (Elenchi) gone.
304 × 215 mm.   Not rubricated.
Binding.   Original boards and clasps; recovered with brown calf and
    elaborate blind tooling in the eighteenth century (?).
Provenance.   At the foot of the first remaining leaf are the arms of Bavaria
    painted in colours with the inscription: 'Iste liber est facultatis Artis
    Studij Ingolstatensis Jo. Altenbek...notarius subscripsit[1].'   On the
    eleventh remaining leaf at the bottom in red ink is written : 'Sapientiam
    atque doctrinam stulti despiciunt. Proverb. 1.'   At the end of the
    colophon : 'Laus Ursule...Johannes Stinn Bidellus Notarius publicus
    subscripsit.'
Hain *1658 (3).   Proctor 1749.   BM.Catalogue II. 361.

---

[1] For another book with the same inscription see BM.Catalogue II. 344 (Ambrosius,
another copy of no. 82 above).

JOHANN SCHÖNSPERGER (1482)

84. JACOBUS DE VORAGINE. Passional Sommerteil. 20 March 1497. F⁰.

> Woodcuts only (see Schreiber), cut out and pasted down. 63 in number, without text. The colouring of these cuts agrees with that of the BM. copy.
> *Binding.* Mounted in a small volume. Brown leather with blind tooling of the fifteenth century, rebacked. Metal centre pieces, corner pieces and clasp, all modern. End-papers of the eighteenth century style.
> *Provenance.* Not recorded.
> Hain 9986. Proctor 1787. BM.Catalogue II. 370. Schreiber 4318.

ERHARD RATDOLT (1487)

85. GUIDO BONATUS. Decem tractatus astrologiae. 26 March 1491. 4⁰.

> *Description* in Hain and BM.Catalogue.
> *Collation,* ✻¹⁴, a–z, A–Z, AA–EE⁸. One leaf (f 8) gone.
> 198 × 155 mm.
> Not rubricated. With decorative woodcut initials. The book contains cuts of the zodiacal signs and the constellations. A few marginal notes (saec. XVI).
> *Binding.* Old brown calf. Red edges.
> *Provenance.* Arms (six hills, in chief three stars) with initials 'A. P. N. P.' of a noble Italian family stamped on the title, and the word 'Pesaresi' twice written. No. 202 in some sale.
> HC. ✻3461. Proctor 1891. BM.Catalogue II. 384. Schreiber 3519.

NUREMBERG

JOHANN SENSENSCHMIDT (1470–1473)

86. FRANCISCUS DE RETZA. Comestorium uitiorum. 1470. Large F⁰.

> *Description* in Hain and BM.Catalogue.
> *Collation* in BM.Catalogue. Blank leaves, 98, 150, 192, 233, gone.

394 × 277 mm.   Large blue capital, with black and gold diaper background, within a purple border, and a conventional floral scroll continued on two sides of the page, on the first leaf.   Ordinary capitals in red or blue. Initial strokes red.   Paragraph marks in red or blue.   Contemporary marginal notes of contents at foot of nearly every page, and at end.
Binding.   Brown calf (XIX cent.).
Provenance.   H. W. Cholmley (1902, with bookplate).
HC. *13884.   Proctor 1942.   BM.Catalogue II. 403.

87.   GERSON (JOHANNES).   De spiritualibus nuptiis.   1470. Small F°.

Description in Hain and BM.Catalogue.
Collation [a–d¹⁰].   Last leaf (blank ?) gone.
284 × 198 mm.   On the first leaf a blue capital on yellow and red diaper. Ordinary capitals in blue or red.   Paragraph marks and initial strokes in red.
Binding.   Morocco by J. B. Hawes, Cambridge.   Gilt edges.
Provenance.   Not recorded.
Hain *7715.   Proctor 1943.   BM.Catalogue II. 403.

88.   CHRYSOSTOMUS.   Sermones de patientia Job.   14 November 1471.   F°.

Translated by Lelius Tifernas.
Description in Hain and BM.Catalogue.
Collation [a¹⁰ bc⁸ d–g¹⁰·¹²].   70 leaves, first and last blank gone.
323 × 229 mm.   Green capital letter on red and blue ground.   Ordinary capitals in blue or red.   Initial strokes red.
At the head of the first leaf is written in a sixteenth century hand ' Anathema sit qui huic opusculo diui Chrisostomi titulum furtim surripuit.'
Fol. 61 *b* (sig. g 4*b*) has an imperfection of printing, on which a note by L. Dodd, 22 Aug. 1877, is inserted.
Binding.   Calf (about 1800).
Provenance.   L. Dodd.   Quaritch.
HC. *5026.   Proctor 1945.   BM.Catalogue II. 405.

89.   HIERONYMUS.   Aureola.   [Ab. 1478 ?]   Small F°.

Description in Hain.
Collation [ab¹⁰ c¹⁰⁺² d⁸].   40 leaves, last two blank.
277 × 195 mm.   Plain red capitals.

S. C.   3

Binding. Modern vellum ; with two leaves of Guido de Baysio, Rosarium decretorum (no. 172), used as fly-leaves.
Provenance. Not recorded.
Hain *8585. Proctor 1956. Panzer I. 244.

JOHANN SENSENSCHMID WITH HEINRICH KEFER (1473)

90. PISIS (RAYNERUS DE). Pantheologia. 1473. Large Fᵒ.

Editio princeps.
Description in Hain and BM.Catalogue.
Collation in BM.Catalogue.
413×283 mm. Third part only; leaves 583–865 (end), but wanting 592, 603, 670, 685, 712, 715-6 and last three leaves (blank). Leaf 808 misplaced, at beginning.
The large decorative initial upon the first page, and the initial V beginning Section V of this book, are only mediocre, with short floral scrolls in red, yellow and green. The ordinary initials are in plain blue or red. Paragraph marks and initial strokes in red. A few marginal notes (saec XV).
Binding. Contemporary white pigskin, with blind tooling. Bosses and clasps have disappeared. A paper label on the side contains an early title :
> ' Tertia.........pantheologie
> ....alphabeti.'

Eight leaves of a poorly written Breviary are pasted down on the inside of the boards and the linings of the quires are from the same source.
Provenance. ' Iste liber est conventus Novaecivitatis ordinis praedicatorum Emptus per fratrem Leonardum Rugff'g... priorem...novaecivitatis. 1471 , (Neustadt an der Aisch?). No. 819 in some sale.
Hain *13015. Proctor 1959. BM.Catalogue II. 405-6.

ANTON KOBERGER (1471)

91. BIBLIA LATINA. 1475. Large Fᵒ.

The first Latin Bible printed by Koberger.
Description in Hain and BM.Catalogue.
Collation in BM.Catalogue and Copinger. Last leaf, blank,'gone.

391 × 273 mm. The large initial on the first leaf has not been executed. Ordinary initials, headlines and paragraph marks plainly rubricated. A few marginal notes in an early sixteenth century hand.

Binding. Modern polished brown morocco by Belz Niedrée.

Provenance. On the first leaf is the superscription 'Canoniae B.V. Mariæ ad Portam Clausam in Griess. Anno 1680.' On the verso of the last leaf is the stencil book-mark of 'Comes Hercules Silva' with his coat of arms. Monogram book-label of Ricardo Heredia, Comte de Benahavis (sale in Paris, 22–30 May 1891). Quaritch. No. 104 in some recent auction.

HC. *3056. Proctor 1970. BM.Catalogue II. 413.

92. PLATINA. Vitae Pontificum. 1481. Small Fᵒ.

Ed. 2.

Description in Hain and BM.Catalogue.

Collation [a¹⁰ b–r⁶ s⁸ t⁶ v⁸]. 128 leaves.

290 × 199 mm. Not rubricated. Marginal notes of the fifteenth century.

Binding. Modern vellum. Gilt edges.

Provenance. Not recorded.

HC. *13047. Proctor 2005. Cf. BM.Catalogue II. 420.

93. BIBLIA GERMANICA. 17 February 1483. Large Fᵒ.

The ninth German Bible. 2 vols.

Description in Hain and BM.Catalogue.

Collation [(Vol. I) *⁴ a–c⁸ d⁶ e–z, A–M⁸ N⁸ O⁶. (Vol. II) P–Z, aa–zz, AA, BB⁸ CC–EE⁶]. In the first volume the last blank leaf has been placed before the coloured cut on fol. v. First and last leaves (blank) of the second volume gone.

371 × 250 mm. The large initials at the beginning of each book are parti-coloured blue and red. The initial to Genesis is blue upon a gold ground now damaged. The parti-coloured initial on folio CCXCVI (the first leaf of the second volume) is slightly more elaborate. The ordinary initials and paragraph marks are plain red.

The woodcuts (110 in number) are the same as those in the Low German Bible, printed by Quentel (Hain *3141, Proctor 1252). The large cut of the Creation on the fifth leaf, and that on the sixth leaf, are strongly but somewhat coarsely coloured.

Binding. Stamped pigskin, stained green (XVI cent.).

Provenance. George Thomas Robinson (bookplates). Quaritch, May 1904 Lot 664 in some sale.

Hain *3137. Proctor 2028. BM.Catalogue II. 424. Schreiber 3461.

94. SCHEDEL (HARTMAN). Liber chronicarum. 12 July 1493. Large Fo.

First Latin edition.
Description in Hain and BM.Catalogue.
Collation in BM.Catalogue. Wants last leaf (blank). The last quire, 'De Sarmacia' supplement, bound after leaf CCLXVI.
438 × 300 mm. Printed ornamental initials. There are 645 different wood-cuts, making with repeats a total of 1809 (S. C. Cockerell), many of which are by Michel Wolgemut, the master of Dürer, and Wilhelm Pleydenwurff.
Binding. Olive brown polished morocco with the Seillière book-stamp.
For other copies see Appendix nos. 278, 279.
For an analysis of the woodcuts see S. C. Cockerell's *Some German Wood-cuts of the Fifteenth Century*, pp. 35-6; and Schreiber.
Provenance. Seillière (1887).
HC. *14508. Proctor 2084. BM.Catalogue II. 437. Schreiber 5203.

JOHANN SENSENSCHMID WITH ANDREAS
FRISNER (1474–1478)

95. THOMAS AQUINAS. Questiones de duodecim quodlibet. 1474. Large Fo.

Description in Hain and BM.Catalogue.
Collation [*² **² (last blank gone), a–c¹⁰ d⁸ e–n¹⁰ o⁴].
400 × 296 mm. Not rubricated. A few marginal notes, by the same hand as in no. 23 with which this is bound.
Binding. With no. 23.
Provenance. Ibid.
Hain *1402. Proctor 2194. Cf. BM.Catalogue II. 406.

96. JUSTINIANUS. Codex. 1475. Large Fo.

Description in Hain and BM.Catalogue.
Collation [*⁴, a–z, A–Q¹⁰ R¹²]. Wants first leaf blank.
Printed in red and black, with rubrication. Ten small woodcuts. On the last leaf of sheet o five lines, on 32b three lines and on sig. A 5 two lines of the text are inserted on a label.
Binding. Original leather with diagonal tooling.
Provenance. From the library of a Carmelite house (qu. at Vienna?). W. H. Crawford (1891). William Morris (1898). Leighton, Catalogue 2835.
Hain *9599. Proctor 2198. BM.Catalogue II. 406–7. Schreiber 4406.

SPEIER

PRINTER OF GESTA CHRISTI (1472)

97. DAMASCENUS (JOHANNES). Liber gestorum Barlaam et Josaphat. [Ab. 1472.] Small F°.

Ed. 2.
Description in Hain and BM.Catalogue.
Collation. a–i^8 k^6.
269 × 193 mm.   Not rubricated.
Binding. Modern half-vellum with paper sides.
Provenance. No trace of ownership, but has been in German hands.
HC. *5914.   Proctor 2319.   BM.Catalogue II. 483.

PETER DRACH (1477)

98. ANTONINUS, Archiepiscopus Florentinus.   Summae theologicae pars secunda.   1477.   F°.

Ed. 2.
Description in Hain.
Collation [a–g^{10} h–m^8 n^6 o–x^{10} y^8 z & ɔ^8 ꝛ ^{10}, aa–ff^{10} gg hh^8 ii^6 kk ll^8 mm^6].
395 × 287 mm.   The large initial on the first leaf finely executed in red and blue with a delicate field of red and green.   The ordinary initials are also well executed in blue or red with gold filigree background.   Paragraph marks in red or blue.   Initial strokes red, and the headlines written in red.
Binding. Contemporary brown leather, rebacked, with diagonal diaper panels, filled with very interesting blind stamps.   (1) The principal one is circular, containing a half length nimbed bishop with mitre and crosier holding a two-spired cathedral in his right hand.   (2) Circular of the crucifixion.   (3) Half length pope with tiara, and cross in the right hand.   (4–6) Rosettes.   (7) Lozenge-shaped, containing half length ecclesiastic with mitre and crosier, and holding a three-spire church in his right hand.   (8) 'Aue-mā.'   (9) Small octagon, containing a quadruped.   The binding is the more interesting as on the flyleaf of the book is the class-mark 'A. 39' with the inscription :

Istum librum legavit fratribus in Wydenbach Dns Johes Lichtenae Capellanus sancti martini minoris colon. pro salute anime sue cuius oratores ipsum propter deum fideles existant.

The 'in wydenbach dominus Johannes' is crossed out in red chalk (XVI cent.).

The book had originally a vellum leaf pasted down at each end, of which a portion remains on the lower cover, containing part of the Hebrew Liturgy (German rite) for the seventh day of Passover (XIX cent.). (Note kindly supplied by Israel Abrahams, M.A.) Over this is pasted a rough woodcut coloured with yellow and red, representing a gallows from which is suspended Nicholaus of Abensperg of lower Bavaria, and his coat of arms with helmet and crest hanging down independently (per bend, argent and sable). Over the cut is handwriting of the fifteenth century :

> 'Nicholaus hrezcu abensperg ben ich genant
> Wem posheit macht mich weid bekant.'

> [Nicholas Abensperg's my name
> Whose wickedness has brought me fame.]

There are the remains of an old paper label on the front cover. The paper has been folded at some time, and it has been doubted whether this is a genuine cut or a reproduction, including the inscription.

Provenance. Quaritch (1902).

Hain *1256. Voulliéme 2000.

ESSLINGEN

CONRAD FYNER (1472)

99. NIGER (PETRUS). Der Stern Meschiah. 20 Dec. 1477. 4°.

Description in Hain. Cf. BM.Catalogue.

Collation [a–c¹⁰ d–z, A–F, aa–ii⁸ kk ll⁶]. In this copy the six preliminary leaves of Hebrew grammar form the penultimate quire, as in Hain.

233 × 163 mm. Hebrew and German. Not rubricated. Simple, good printed initial letters. Traces of manuscript signatures remain. A few marginal notes (some in Hebrew) of the sixteenth century.

There are two good full-page woodcuts in the book, one (on the first leaf) of the author, standing in conversation with a group of five men also standing, the other on the ninth leaf (facing the first treatise) of Christ's entry into Jerusalem.

Binding. Original pigskin, panel with five stamps. Metal clasps.

Provenance. Old library label on back in red $\frac{E}{265}$. Bookplate of Karl Becher, M.D., of Karlsbad.

Hain *11886. Proctor 2464. Voulliéme 1138. Cf. BM.Catalogue II. 516. Schreiber 5217.

100. GUIDO DE MONTE ROCHERII. Manipulus Curatorum. [Ab. 1478.] Small Fº.

Description in Hain and BM.Catalogue.
Collation [a¹⁰ b–q⁸].
271 × 200 mm. Rubricated. Plain red painted initials. A few contemporary marginal notes.
Binding. Modern bright red morocco with elaborate showy gilt tooling. Gilt edges. Qu. Budapest?
Provenance. Label of Dörner Adam, bookseller and bookbinder of Budapest.
HC. *8158. Proctor 2480. BM.Catalogue II. 516.

101. JACOBUS DE THERAMO. Belial. [Ab. 1475.] Small Fº.

German.
Description in Copinger.
Collation in Copinger. Leaves 50–58 gone.
262 × 202 mm. Rubricated. Plain red painted initial letters. Rough woodcuts, apparently from the first Strassburg edition (cf. Schorbach-Spirgatis, *Knoblochtzer*, p. 1).
Binding. Modern half-vellum binding, with paper sides.
Provenance. On the first page is the inscription 'ex bibl. Jeisachiorum (?) 1809.' W. H. Dutton (1904), with bookplate. Bought through Leighton.
Copinger 5804. Schreiber 4282.

ULM

JOHANN ZAINER (1473–1487)

102. ALBERTUS MAGNUS. Opus de misterio missae. 29 May 1473. Fº.

The first edition.
Description in Hain and BM.Catalogue.
Collation in B.M.Catalogue and Morgan.
293 × 205 mm. Three lines of the capital ℞ (each line ending with an M). Fol. 5–42, simple woodcut initials painted red ; the rest rubricated only. The first leaf of the text has the printed floral (columbine) border on two sides, painted in red and blue.
A smaller size of paper used in two sections.
Three lines of the capital ℞ (each ending with an M) used as furniture at end and some more on fol. 4 *b*.

Binding. Bound in two leaves of a manuscript missal of about the year 1500.

Provenance. R. B. Stewart (1888) with bookplate (Lot 306). No. 528 in some recent collection.

Hain *449. Proctor 2494. Morgan, no. 193. BM.Catalogue II. 520.

103. DURANDUS (GULIELMUS). Rationale diuinorum officiorum. 1473. Large F°.

Description in Hain and BM.Catalogue.

Collation [a^{12} b–g^{10} h^{8+1} i–z, & ɔ^{10} 2 ^{8} 2 2 ^{10}].

394 × 270 mm. The large initial letter on the first leaf of the text is printed; and two sides of the margin are covered with a woodcut floral scroll, containing the figure of a jester. Plainly rubricated.

Binding. Plain vellum (saec. XIX).

Provenance. The inscription 'FF. Lorelhausensium' (?) at the foot of the first page (saec. XVII).

HC. *6474. Proctor 2498. BM.Catalogue II. 521–2.

JOHANN REGER (1486–1499)

104. PTOLEMAEUS. Geographia. 21 July 1486. Large F°.

The Latin translation of Jacobus Angelus.

Description in Hain and BM.Catalogue.

Collation. AB^8 C^{10} DE^8 a^{10} b–i^8. 32 unnumbered maps (= 32 sheets). a–c^8.

413 × 290 mm. Woodcut initials. The large maps coloured in brown, red, and occasionally green.

Binding. Dark brown modern morocco, with blind tooling, and the arms of William Tennant of Little Aston Hall, Shenstone, Stafford, in gold. Bound by C. Lewis.

Provenance. Tennant.

HC. *13540. Proctor 2580. BM.Catalogue II. 540. Schreiber 5032.

EICHSTÄTT

MICHAEL REYSER (1488)

105. BRUNO, Episcopus Herbipolensis. Super psalterium. [Ab. 1485.] Small F°.

Description in Hain, Morgan.

Collation in Morgan [**⁸ a⁸ b–z & 9, A–F⁸·⁶ G⁸ H–L⁸·⁶ M⁸ N¹⁰]. 280 leaves.
Sig. G 5, N 10, both blank, cut away.

293 × 212 mm. Finely illuminated gold initial letters to Pss. i, xxvi, xxxviii,
li, lii, lxviii, lxxx, xcvii, cix. Red initial strokes in the first nine leaves
only.

Binding. Stamped pigskin (cf. Morgan copy). Metal clasps and knobs,
all gone. With vesica-shaped impression of seal on the front board,
consisting of a standing figure of St Peter holding a large key in the
right hand, aureole, diaper background ; surrounded by legend :
S(igillum) Iohannis ...... monasterii : sti : Petri : erfordens (?) :

Four vellum leaves from a German missal (XII cent.) as end papers. On
the second :

Istud psalterium comparavit M. Joh. Milbach anno xpi 1489 Quod legavit
monasterio montissancti petri in erffordia Anno dni M. ccccc. lxxxxii.

Also : 'Liber scti petri apli in erffordia.' Class-mark I. XVI. Later ;
'Liber SS. Petri et Pauli Erpho.'

Provenance. ' As above (1489).

Bought of ' Ellis May 15, 1867.' H. W. Cholmley, 26 November 1902, lot 982.

HC. *4011. Proctor 3123. Morgan, no. 215.

ITALY

ROME

CONRAD SWEYNHEYM AND ARNOLD PANNARTZ (1467)

106. APULEIUS. Opera. 27 February 1469. F°.

Editio princeps.
Description in Hain, Morgan.
Collation in Morgan. [a⁶, b–o¹⁰, pq¹², r¹⁰ s⁸.] Last leaf blank, gone.
312 × 220 mm. Not rubricated. Marginal notes in a hand of about the
    year 1500.
Binding. Modern vellum binding.
Provenance. Archinto, of Milan (1863), bookplate. Bookplate and sig-
    nature of the 26th Earl of Crawford.
HC. *1314. Proctor 3297. Morgan, no. 241. Duff, p. 30.

107. CICERO. Epistolae ad Brutum, etc. 1470. F°.

Editio princeps.
Description in Hain.
Collation [A–E¹⁰ F¹² G–K¹⁰ L⁸ M–V¹⁰]. 200 leaves, last blank.
323 × 224 mm. Not rubricated. Marginal notes of about 1500 on the first
    few leaves have been partially washed out.
Binding. Modern russia binding, rebacked with morocco.
Provenance. Duke of Sussex, with bookplate.
HC. *5213. Proctor 3311. Duff, p. 30.

ULRICH HAN (1468)

108. JUVENALIS. Satirae. [Ab. 1470.] 4°.

Description in Hain.
Collation [a⁸ b¹² c⁸ d–g¹⁰· ⁶ h¹⁰ i⁸⁺¹]. Collated by Gilbert Ellis.
222 × 158 mm. A plain initial S in red overlaid in gold on the first leaf.
   Initials of the other satires in plain red or blue. A good untouched
   copy.
Binding. Dark blue Harleian style, heavily tooled (with 109).
Provenance. Sunderland sale (1881), No. 7026. Bought by Ellis and
   White.
Hain 9660. Spencer *Bibl. Spencer.* II. 117.

109. PERSIUS. Satirae. [Ab. 1470.] 4°.

Description in Hain.
Collation [ab⁸]. First and last blank.
222 × 158 mm.
Binding. With no. 108.
Provenance. See no. 108.
H. 12714. Spencer, *Bibl. Spencer.* II. 219.

JOHANNES PHILIPPI DE LIGNAMINE (1470)

110. NURSIA (BENEDICTUS DE). Libellus de conservatione
sanitatis, &c. 1475. 4°.

With Tadeus de Florentia De regimine sanitatis, and epistle to Sixtus IV
   by the printer.
Description in Hain.
Collation [a² b–i¹⁰ k⁸ l–p¹⁰]. Last leaf (blank?) gone.
211 × 142 mm. Much water-stained. Parts of the first three leaves have
   perished, and there are other small mutilations. A crude large initial
   letter in blue and red at the commencement of the text on the eighth leaf.
   Ordinary initials in plain blue or red.
Binding. Half bound in common brown leather with paper sides (eighteenth
   century), red and blue labels.
Provenance. An old library printed book-label within a decorative border
   contains the number

II	
E	5
4	

Nos. 20566 and 69746 in some previous lists. Bought of Rosenthal.
Hain *11919. Proctor 3397A.

VENICE

WENDELIN OF SPEIER (1470)

111. CICERO. De officiis, etc.   13 August 1470.   Large 4º.

The first book printed by Wendelin of Speier.

Contains: De officiis, Paradoxa, De amicitia, De senectute, Somnium Scipionis and Versus XII Sapientum.

Description in Hain (132 leaves); Copinger (133 leaves); Pellechet (136 leaves).

Collation [a¹⁰ b–m⁸ n¹⁰ o–q⁸ r⁴] 136 leaves. One blank leaf at beginning, and two blank leaves at end, wanting.

286 × 198 mm. Not rubricated. A few initials painted in plain red. The first leaf is elaborately illuminated, with a decorative border painted on three sides in gold, blue, red, green and purple[1]. At the foot a centaur carrying a nude woman and child, with the arms of the family on the left and the initial Z on the right. The first initial letter Q with the white vine tracery is elaborately coloured. This copy agrees with Hain's variety as against that indicated by Copinger.

Binding. Red morocco with plain gold tooling (about 1800) by Mrs Weir (Wodhull Cat.).

Provenance. (XV cent.) Coat of arms: vert, a lion rampant holding a tree. The Wodhull copy with signature, bought by him at Edwards's sale in 1791. Bought at Wodhull's sale in 1886 by Quaritch (collated by Alb. Müller). Lot 709.

HC. 5257 (first variety). Proctor 4020. Pellechet-Polain 3728.

NICOLAS JENSON (1470)

112. JUSTINUS. Epitome historiarum Trogi Pompeii. 1470. 4º.

Editio princeps.

Description in Hain.

Collation [a–o¹⁰].

278 × 185 mm. Plain initial letters in red or blue surrounded with decorative pen-work. On the first page is an elaborate border upon two sides with interlacing work on a green ground, and an elaborated C of the same character on a gold ground.

Binding. Red morocco with gilt tooling (eighteenth century).

Provenance. Earl of Jersey, Osterley Park (1885), with bookplate.

Hain 9647. Proctor 4067.

---

[1] The ornament in the upper margin and the initial Q are painted over impressions from engraved blocks. See A. W. Pollard in *Bibliographia* III. 122–128.

113. SUETONIUS. Vitae Caesarum. 1471. 4°.

Ed. 3.

Description in Hain (162 leaves only).

Collation [a–m$^{10\cdot 12}$ no^{10} p^{12}] 164 leaves. Last blank.

270×190 mm. Plain initials in red or blue in the first sheets only : but on the first leaf is an elaborate border of filigree work upon red and blue ground on two sides. Good initial letters to each book. At the foot a fillet containing the arms: or a bend azure. A few marginal notes (saec. XV).

Binding. Harleian red morocco with gold tooling, rebacked.

Provenance. (See above.) Harleian copy. Charles Chauncy (1790) with bookplate and signature. Duke of Grafton. Hibbert. Sold by Ellis 16 May 1867.

Hain *15117. Proctor 4070.

114. CICERO. Tusculanae Quaestiones. 1472. 4°.

Description in Hain, Pellechet.

Collation [a^{10} b–g^8 h^6 i–l^8] 88 leaves. Wants first leaf blank, and two blank leaves at end.

279×198 mm. Not rubricated.

Binding. Plain red morocco (early XIX cent.).

Provenance. Hamilton Palace (1884), lot 549.

Hain *5313. Proctor 4088. Pellechet-Polain 3778.

115. PLINIUS SECUNDUS (GAIUS). Historia Naturale. 1476. F°.

The Italian translation of Cristoforo Landino.

Description in Hain.

Collation in Chawner. [a–x^{10}, y–3, A–C^8 D–N^{10} O^{10} (fol. 10 cancelled) P^{10} Q^8 RS^{10} T^8 V^{10}.]

This copy wants first and last leaves blank; sig. h 4 and 7 are wanting, and replaced by duplicates of sig. n 4 and 7; and sheets T and V are misbound. Leaves at the beginning inlaid.

422×285 mm. Some large initials painted in red and blue, or crimson and green, or violet and green. Gold initials with white vine ornamentation at the beginning of Books II, III, V, VIII, XII, XIV, XV, XVI, XVIII, XXII, XXIV, XXV, XXXVI.

Jewel-work initials before Books XX, XXI, XXVII, XXIX (with profile cameo). Some rubrication.

Binding. Italian mottled vellum (eighteenth century).

Provenance. No. 10959 in some collection.

Hain *13105 (first variant). Proctor 4099. Chawner 55.

FRANZ RENNER, WITH NICOLAUS OF FRANKFORT (1473)

116. MARCHESINUS (JOANNES). Mammotrectus. 1476. 4°.

Description. Cf. Hain-Copinger.
Collation. A–C⁸, a¹⁰ b–y, i, z, 3⁸⁺¹. 269 leaves.
Wants A–C⁸, and last leaf containing tabula.
202 × 146 mm. Capitals in red, slightly decorative. Paragraph marks in red.
Binding. Red morocco (XVIII cent.) rebacked.
Provenance. Not recorded.
HC. 10557 (incorrect). Proctor 4168.

JOHANN OF COLOGNE WITH JOHANN MANTHEN (1474–1480)

117. PRISCIANUS. Opera Grammatica. 1476. F°.

Description in HC.
Collation in Copinger. With blank first leaf.
324 × 230 mm. Some initials parti-coloured in red and blue. Rubricated in Germany.
Binding. Old French citron morocco.
Provenance. At the foot of the first leaf are the initials ' P. G.,' and on the last leaf the autograph ' M. Brittij de Cilia.' (Cilli in Styria.) Duke of Grafton ' 1782' (1815). Cholmley (1902).
HC. *13357. Proctor 4306.

118. ARISTOTELES. De animalibus. Interprete Theodoro Gaza. 1476. Small F°.

First dated edition of the Latin translation.
Description in Hain.
Collation [ab¹⁰ c⁸ d–l⁸· ¹⁰ m–t¹⁰ u⁸ x¹⁰, aa–dd¹⁰ ee⁸ ff⁶]. First and last eaves, blank, gone.
295 × 204 mm. Rubricated in red or blue. Initial strokes red.
Binding. Handsome red morocco with dentelle tooling, inlaid with black and green.
Provenance. J. B. Huzard (1842) i, 2429. Yemeniz copy with label (1867) no. 484. Cholmley sale (1902), lot 206.
HC. *1699. Proctor 4312.

119. LACTANTIUS. Opera. 27 August 1478. Small Fº.

Description in Hain.
Collation. a¹² b–m¹⁰ n⁸ o–r¹⁰ s–x⁸ y¹⁰ z⁸ [ ]⁸. Wants a 1, blank. Misbound
at end.
272 × 200 mm. The principal initials in gold on coloured ground with star
ornament in the margin, probably Ferrarese or Paduan work; others
with the white vine background. Ordinary initials in plain red or blue.
A few marginal notes of the fifteenth century.
Binding. Plain Italian vellum.
Provenance. The first leaf of text, in the illuminated escutcheon at foot,
has the representation of a monstrance.
HC. *9814. Proctor 4332.

ERHARD RATDOLT (1476)

120. ROLEWINCK. Fasciculus Temporum. 24 November
1480. Small Fº.

Description in Hain, Redgrave, D'Essling.
Collation in Redgrave and D'Essling. First leaf blank gone.
292 × 205 mm. Not rubricated. Woodcuts and printed initial letters. Marginal notes.
Binding. Plain brown calf, with gold tooling on the back, and red edges
(eighteenth century).
Provenance. On the second leaf (the first of the Tabula) the red bookstamp 'Ex Bibliot. Dom: P: Dubrowsky. Nº. .' The signature of
'Burelli' pasted on the corner of a flyleaf. The Earl of Westmorland
(1887), with label 1856.
HC. *6926. Redgrave 17. Proctor 4379. Essling 277.

121. EUCLIDES. Elementa. 25 May 1482. Fº.

Editio princeps.
Description in Hain, Redgrave, D'Essling.
Collation in Redgrave and Chawner.
300 × 212 mm. Not rubricated. A woodcut border round three sides of the
first leaf of the text, painted yellow, as also the background of the printed
initial letter, which is painted red.
Binding. Half brown calf, brown paper sides.
Provenance. The medallion in the foot of the border contains a coat of
arms: gules, a lion's jamb (qu. Caccia?) or and in chief a pear-shape
charge not identified.

On the flyleaf is the inscription: 'Bibliothecae Cappucinorum Bergomi Fr. Faustinus a Bergomo Cappuccinus.' The copy afterwards became the property, about 1855, of the Malta Protestant College, and contains their embossed stamp. Modern bookplate of 'FS.' Collated for Quaritch in 1880.

HC. *6693. Redgrave 26. Proctor 4383. Essling 282. Chawner.

122. POMPONIUS MELA. Cosmographia. 18 July 1482. 4°.

Description in Hain.
Collation in Redgrave. A–F⁸.
210×152 mm. With map of the world on verso of first leaf. Woodcut initials.
Binding. Modern half-vellum with paper sides.
Provenance. Not recorded.
HC. *11019. Proctor 4385. Redgrave 28. Essling 274.

123. REGIOMONTANUS (JOHANNES). Kalendarium. 9 August 1482. 4°.

Printed for Joannes Lucius Santritter. Regiomontanus is the literary name of Müller.
Description in Hain.
Collation in Redgrave [a¹⁰ bc⁸ d²].
185×140 mm. Red and black printing. Large red initial on first page, and black border with white scroll work. This is badly cut into at foot.
Binding. Modern white half-vellum, with parchment sides. On the verso of the last leaf a strip of metal is affixed.
Provenance. Not recorded.
HC. *13777. Proctor 4386. Redgrave 29.

124. PUBLICIUS (JACOBUS). Artis oratoriae epitome; ars epistolaris; et ars memoriae. 30 November 1482. 4°.

Description in Hain.
Collation in Copinger, Redgrave, etc.
208 × 145 mm. Nine pages of woodcuts (the last with index affixed); also cut of chessboard on the last leaf.
Binding. Old Italian vellum.
Provenance. Not recorded.
HC. *13545. Proctor 4388. Redgrave 31. Essling 292. Chawner 69.

125. ALFONSUS, Rex Hispaniae. Tabulae Astronomicae.
4 July 1483. 4°.

Description in Hain and Essling.
Collation in Redgrave, Essling. a–l⁸ m⁶. Wants first leaf blank.
224 × 165 mm. Text-title in red. Large printed initials. Two diagrams
of eclipses. Some marginal notes (saec. XV–XVI).
Binding. Modern half-parchment. Mottled paper sides.
Provenance. Not recorded.
HC. *868. Proctor 4389. Redgrave 34. Essling 302.

126. SACRO BOSCO (JOHANNES DE). Sphaera Mundi. 1485. 4°.

Description in Hain, etc.
Collation in Redgrave, Essling.
195 × 140 mm. With sixty-one diagrams in black, red, and two shades of
brown. This copy reads 'ADOLFSCENTIBUS' as Hain, not as in
Essling.
Binding. Modern half-vellum. Paper sides.
Provenance. Not recorded.
HC. *114111. Proctor 4402. Redgrave 57. Essling 259.

PETRUS DE PIASIIS (1479)

127. DANTE. Divina Commedia, col commento di Cristoforo
Landino. 18 November 1491. F°.

Description in HC., Essling.
Collation in Essling. Four leaves of table (sig. AA⁴), bound at end.
303 × 198 mm. Woodcuts at the head of the first six cantos of the Inferno,
coloured. Woodcut initials. On the first blank page is a manuscript
'Alphabetum lusorum videlicet eorum peccatorum qui committuntur in
ludo.' A few marginal notes.
Binding. Modern red morocco, by Leighton.
Provenance. Not recorded.
HC. 5950. Proctor 4482. Essling 532. Fiske I. 5.

OCTAVIANUS SCOTUS (1480–1484)

128. DANTE. La Divina Commedia col commento di Cristoforo
Landino. 23 March 1484. F° (parts of sig. z and & 4°).

Description in HC., Fiske.
Collation in Copinger.
325 × 229 mm. Initial letters in plain red. A few initial strokes yellow.
The woodcut initials also coloured.

Binding. Plain Italian vellum.
Provenance. On the first page is the inscription 'Furij (?) Lupi et ami-
corum' (saec. XVI). Sir T. D. Gibson-Carmichael (1903), with bookplate,
lot 2789.
HC. 5947. Proctor 4581. Fiske I. 5.

THOMAS DE BLAVIS (1481)

129. HYGINUS. Poeticon Astronomicon. 7 June 1488. 4°.

Description in HC., Essling.
Collation. a–g⁸.
207 × 155 mm. Large and small initial letters in black. Woodcuts of the
constellations and planets.
Binding. Modern half-vellum. Paper sides.
Provenance. Not recorded.
HC. *9065. Proctor 4765. Essling 287.

ANDREAS DE BONETIS (1483)

130. AUGUSTINUS. Opuscula. 23 July 1484. 4°.

Ed. 2.
Description in HC.
Collation. a–z, & ɔ ⁊ , A–F⁸ G⁴ H–K⁸ L⁴. Wants a 1 (not seen).
209 × 148 mm. Plain scrolled initials and paragraph marks in blue or
red; red initial strokes.
Binding. Black morocco (saec. XIX).
Provenance. Royal Society (bookplate), sale (1872).
HC. *1947. Proctor 4813.

BERNARDINUS BENALIUS (1483)

131. FORESTI (JACOBO PHILIPPO). Supplementum chronicarum. 15 December 1486. F°.

Description in Hain, Essling.
Collation. a⁸ b⁴ c–l⁸ m⁶ n–p, A–U⁸.
295 × 195 mm. Printed initial letters and woodcuts.
Binding. Brown marbled calf (eighteenth century).
Provenance. Formerly belonging to Tongerloo ('Bibl. Tong.'), and to
' J. Loreuoirls ' (?).

131 A. ——. Another copy.

288 x 206 mm. Rubricated.

Binding. Formerly bound in brown calf with a crowned D in the centre of each board. Rebound in 1895 in half-calf with paper sides.

Provenance. The signature of Francis Wrangham, Archdeacon of Cleveland, on the flyleaf, and an inscription recording the gift of the book to the Rev. Charles Kerry by the Rev. E. H. Knowles, M.A., late Michel Fellow of Queen's College, Oxford, June 12, 1863 (Canon of Rochester †1899). Bought of Quaritch in April 1904.

HC. *2807. Proctor 4868. Essling 342.

BONETUS LOCATELLUS (1487)

132. SACRO BOSCO (JOHANNES DE). Sphaera Mundi. 4 October 1490. 4°.

For Octavianus Scotus, with his mark in red at end.

Description in Hain, Essling.

Collation. a–f⁸.

213 × 156 mm.

Cut of Astronomia on verso of first leaf, and numerous diagrams, some colour-printed in brown and red. Large crudely-cut 12-line and 4-line initial letters.

Some marginal notes (saec. XVII) in a minute hand.

Binding. Boards covered with marbled paper.

Provenance. Bought of Leighton (1905 Catalogue), no. 275.

HC. *14113. Proctor 5023. Essling 261.

JOHANN HAMMAN, OR HERZOG (1490)

133. ALFONSUS, Rex Hispaniae. Tabulae Astronomicae. 31 October 1492. 4°.

Description in Hain.

Collation. A–D⁸ e⁶, a–h⁸ ik⁶.

205 × 153 mm. 8-line, 6-line, and 5-line initial letters, and some left blank for rubrication. No woodcuts. A few marginal notes (saec. XVI).

Binding. Paper.

Provenance. Signature 'Philippi Ubaldini Ripæ Florentini' and MS. note: 'Habui Pisis die 19 Xbris an. 1711 a quodam extero librario prope Ecclesiam Monasterij S^{ti} Michaelis Monachorum Camaldulensium pretio duorum Juliorum fr. Salu' Ascanio Ord. Pred.' Stamp of S. Maria Novella, Florence, 'No. 334.'

Hain *869. Proctor 5188.

134. REGIOMONTANUS (JOHANNES). Epitoma in Almagestum Ptolomei. 31 August 1496. F⁰.

> With G. Purbachius. Edited by Caspar Grossch and Stephen Roemer [and J. B. Abiosus].
> *Description* in HC., Essling.
> *Collation*, ibid. a¹⁰ as in Essling, not as HC. Wants last leaf blank.
> 304 × 211 mm. Woodcut initials and marginal diagrams.
> *Binding.* Plain Italian vellum.
> *Provenance.* Not recorded.
> HC. *13806. Proctor 5197. Essling 895.

PHILIPPUS PINCIUS (1490)

135. LIVIUS. Historiae Romanae Decades. 3 November 1495. F⁰.

> *Description* in HC., Essling, etc.
> *ollation.* A⁸ a⁸ b⁴ c–l⁸ mn¹⁰, A–K⁸ L¹⁰, aa–ii⁸.
> 320 × 215 mm.
> Preceded by the Epistle of John bishop of Aleria to Pope Paul II and to Marco Cardinal of St Mark. The first leaf of the text of each Decade is contained in a large woodcut border and has a large illustration. The text has woodcut initials and 171 small woodcuts.
> Many marginal notes (saec. XVI).
> *Binding.* Green half-roan by Staderini of Rome.
> *Provenance.* Before the text on the verso of the first leaf is the MS. note, 'Liber Illustrissimi Domini Alexandri de Bonis.' Library mark 'o. vi. 5.'
> HC. *10141. Proctor 5308. Brunet III. 1103. Essling 34.

BARTHOLOMAEUS DE ZANIS (1491)

136. PETRARCA. Trionfi, sonetti e canzoni col commento di Francesco Filelfo. 11 July—30 August 1497. F⁰.

> Corrected by Gabriele Bruno and Ieronimo Cento.
> *Description* in HC., Essling.
> *Collation.* aa⁸, a–q⁸, A–L⁸ M¹⁰.
> 282 × 200 mm. Two large woodcut initials and a few small ones. Whole-page woodcuts of the Triumphs of Chastity, Death, Fame, Time, and Divinity.
> This copy wants the first eight leaves containing the prologue and full-page cut of the Triumph of Love.
> *Binding.* Common half-roan.
> *Provenance.* Olschki, Venice, label at end.
> HC. *12776. Proctor 5339. Essling 81.

PETRUS DE QUARENGIIS (1492)

137. PETRARCA (FRANCESCO). Trionfi col commento di Francesco Filelfo e di Bernardo Ilicino. 12 January 1492. F°.

Part I only, containing the Trionfi.
Description. Fol. 1 blank. F. 2. Per informatione & dechiaratione di questa | Tabula *etc.* F. 6 *b.* Prologus. F. 8 *b.* Woodcut. Text, numbered pages I–CXXVIII. Fol. 128 *b.* Finit Petrarcha nuper summa diligētia a reuerendo. P. ordinis minorū magistro Gabriele bruno uene|to terræ sanctæ ministro emendatus anno domini. M.cccc.lxxxxxii. (*sic*) die .xii. Ianuarii. | Registrum etc.
Collation. aa⁸, a–q⁸. Wants sig. o 6, p 7.
314×205 mm. Four whole-page woodcuts (Love, Fame, Death, Chastity). (Cuts of Fame and Chastity have been transposed by the printer.) These cuts are from the Venetian edition of 1488. White vine initial on fol. 1, and the arms of the original owner, emblazoned in colour at foot: sable, on a bend sinister azure, three stars or. Within a wreath containing the initials N.M.
Binding. Modern brown morocco, by Leighton.
Provenance. See above. J. and J. Leighton (1905), no. 3940.
Essling 80.

ALDUS MANUCIUS (1495)

138. ARISTOTELES. Opera Graecé. Vol. I. 1 November 1495. F°.

Editio princeps.
Description in Hain.
Collation in Essling, Chawner.
314×210 mm. Numerous marginal notes, written about 1500, in Latin and Greek by a scholar of distinction.
Binding. Modern half-vellum, Italian.
Provenance. R. B. Stewart (1888) with bookplate.
HC. *1657 (1). Proctor 5547. Chawner 102. Essling 862.

139. ASTRONOMICI VETERES. October 1499. F°.

Editio princeps.
Description in Hain, Essling.
Collation in Essling. Sig. c 2 and 9 wanting.
310×210 mm. Initial letters in plain blue or red. Thirty-nine woodcuts in the Aratus.

Binding. Fine olive morocco (sixteenth century), with rich gold tooling and cameos on both boards. Painted edges. Rebacked. Aldine stamp (XIX cent.) on sides as in no. 211.

Provenance. On the first leaf is the MS. note: 'Camill falconer, aggreg. Lugd, Natal'. fili, Andr. nepos 1693.'

T. Crofts (1783). Syston Park (1884) with bookplates.

HC. *14559. Proctor 5570. Essling 1186.

140. COLONNA (FRANCISCUS). Poliphili Hypnerotomachia. December 1499. F°.

Editio princeps.
Description in Hain.
Collation. [ ]⁴, a–y⁸ z¹⁰, A–E⁸ F⁴. Wants last leaf.
302 × 210. Numerous woodcuts.
Binding. Plain vellum.
Provenance. Earl of Aylesford (1888) with bookplate.
For other copies see Appendix nos. 301 and 302.
HC. *5501. Proctor 5574. Essling 1198. Chawner 102.

FERRARA

LORENZO ROSSI (1489)

141. FORESTI (JACOBO FILIPPO). De claris mulieribus. 29 April 1497. F°.

Description in HC., Morgan.
Collation. A⁴, a–e⁸ f⁶ g–p⁸ q–x⁶·⁸ yz⁶.
302·5 × 196 mm. Printed initial letters and woodcuts; engraved title, two engraved frontispieces, and first leaf of the text within an elaborate border. Marginal notes of the seventeenth century in an Italian hand-writing.
Binding. Pink morocco with gold tooling (nineteenth century).
Provenance. On the second leaf are three inscriptions (1) 'Frater Basilius …v.g. de Ripa manu propria,' (2) 'Sancti Barnabe ad usum fratris Adeodati de claris,' (3) 'Bibliothecæ S. Barnabæ Brixiæ.' Syston Park (1884) with both bookplates.
HC. *2813. Proctor 5762. F. Lippmann, *Wood-engraving*, p. 153. Morgan II. 107 (no. 382).

142. HIERONYMUS. Vita e Epistole. 12 October 1497. F°.

Italian translation by Fra Matheo da Ferrara.
Description in Morgan, Hain (imperfect). On fol. 5 b in place of the inscription 'Herculis' &c. is a cut of St Jerome.

Collation. [✳]⁴ a¹⁰–m⁸ n o⁶ p–q⁸ r–y⁸·⁶ z & 9 𝒰, A–N⁶.

310×220 mm. Woodcut title. White vine woodcut initials. Numerous woodcuts. On fol. 2 *b*, 5 *b*, 6 *a* are whole-page woodcut borders.

Binding. Modern crimson morocco, with gold tooling, by Leighton. A letter from Mr Quaritch inserted, on the Gaisford and Cosens copies, with other notes.

For another state see Appendix no. 303.

Provenance. F. W. Cosens (1890). Leighton (cf. his catalogue 1905, no. 2506).

Hain 8566. Proctor 5765. F. Lippmann, *op. cit.*, p. 154. Cf. Morgan II. no. 383.

MILAN

ANTONIUS ZAROTUS (1471)

143. HORATIUS. Opera. 16 March 1474. Large 4º.

First dated edition.

Description in HC.

Collation. (Carmina) [a–f¹⁰ (f 10 blank gone)]. (De arte poetica) [g⁸]. (Sermones) [h–k¹⁰ l⁴ (l 4 blank gone)]. Epistolae [mn¹⁰ o⁶] (o 5 and 6 gone, blank?).

270×188 mm. Not rubricated. A few unimportant marginal notes (sixteenth century).

Binding. Purple morocco with gold line by C. Lewis. Bound with no. 144.

Provenance. Bought of Payne and Foss in 1829. Syston Park (1884) with both bookplates. Lord Crawford (1889), lot 502.

HC. ✳8876 (1). Proctor 5779.

144. ACRON. Commentarius in Horatium. 13 August 1474. 4º.

Description in Hain.

Collation. [a–o¹⁰ p⁸] 148 leaves. First leaf (blank) gone.

270×188 mm. Not rubricated.

Binding. See no. 143.

Provenance. Ibid.

Hain 8876 (2). Proctor 5783.

145. PETRARCA (FRANCESCO). Trionfi, Sonetti e Canzoni col commento di F. Filelfo e di B. Ilicini. 1 August 1494. Fº.

Description in Copinger.

Collation. (Trionfi) aa⁸ a–q⁸. (Sonetti) A–M⁸ N⁶. First and last leaves gone (both blank?).

292 × 214 mm. Woodcut initials, and six whole-page illustrations. Mr Cockerell points out that the cuts illustrating the Triumphs of Death, Time, and Divinity appear to be metal cuts by a Spanish hand. A few marginal notes.

Binding. Half-vellum (eighteenth century).

Provenance. Leighton catalogue (1905), no. 3941.

Hain 12762. Proctor 5836. Copinger 4706. Cf. Essling 79 note.

BONUS ACCURSIUS (1478)

146. PSALTERIUM GRAECO-LATINUM. 20 September 1481. 4°.

Editio princeps. With dedicatory epistle by John of Piacenza, a monk, to the Bishop of Bergamo.

Description in Hain.

Collation. [❊]⁶, a–x⁸ y, z⁶.

268 × 195 mm. Only the first seven leaves rubricated.

Binding. Modern dark olive morocco with gold tooling and gilt edges.

Provenance. Bought of Quaritch in 1867.

HC. ❊13454. Proctor 5966.

ULRICH SCINZENZELER

147. PETRARCA. Trionfi e Sonetti (10 Feb.). 26 March 1494. F°.

With commentary of Bernardo Ilicini and Francesco Filelfo. Sonetti only.

Description in Hain.

Collation. Trionfi (not seen). Sonetti A–M⁸ N⁶. Last leaf blank gone.

276 × 203 mm.

Binding. Paper.

Provenance. William Powell of Dublin (signature and bookplate).

HC. 12775. Chawner 120.

FLORENCE

NICOLAUS LAURENTII (1477)

148. BERLINGHIERI (FRANCESCO). Geographia. [1481.] Large F°.

A versification in terza rima of the Cosmographia of Ptolemy, dedicated to Federigo Duke of Urbino.

Description in Hain.

Collation. [❊]² aa¹⁰ bb–dd⁸ ee⁶ ff, gg⁸ hh⁶ [ii]⁴, a⁶ b¹⁰ c⁸ d, e¹² f¹⁰+31 maps (on 30 double leaves).

The following description of this copy by the Earl of Crawford was printed
in the sale catalogue of 1887:

'The original title is printed in black on the *verso* of folio 1. At a later
period the following title was printed in red on the *recto* of the same folio:

GEOGRAPHIA DI | FRANCESCO BERLINGHIERI | FIORENTINO IN TERZA |
RIMA ET LINGVA TOSCANA DI|STINCTA CON LE SVE TAVO|LE IN
VARII SITI ET PRO|VINCIE SECONDO LA | GEOGRAPHIA | ET DISTIN|
ctione dele | tauole di Ptolomeo | Cum gratia & Priuilegio. |

On the *verso* of this leaf is printed:

IN QVE|STO VOLVME | SI CONTENGONO SEP|TE GIORNATE DELLA GEOG|
RAPHIA DI FRANCESCO BERLIN|GERI FIORENTINO ALLO IL|LUSTRISSIMO
FEDERI|GO DUCA DUR|BINO.

At the foot of fol. f. 10 the Registro is printed:

Impresso infirenze per Nicolo Todescho | & emendato con summa dili|
gentia dallo auctore. |

There is no doubt but that this registro was printed at the same time that
the *red* title was struck, and on the leaf which was originally blank.
Brunet is wrong in saying that this folio was substituted for the blank, as
in this, my best copy it is part of the leaf f. 1. These additions to the
" Remainder" were probably made about 1520–25.'

407 × 274 mm. Only one initial letter (that on the third leaf) has been
illuminated. On this page the large initial G is in plain gold, with a
rich background in red and blue with filigree work in white and yellow.
There is also a rich floral scroll extending half the length of the in-
terior margin. Thirty-one maps engraved on copper, including one of
the world with the twelve winds, supposed to have been printed prior
to those of B. Baldini for the Dante of 1481, and closely resembling the
figures in the Monte-Sancto published in Florence in 1478 by the printer
of Berlinghieri. Some of the maps are slightly tinged with colour. For
a full description of these plates see Justin Winsor *Bibliography of
Ptolemy's Geography*, p. 4 (Harvard Bibliographies, Vol. I. No. 18,
1884). The first has been cut into at the sides.

Binding. Vellum (XIX century).

Provenance. On the title-page is the inscription 'Collegij Regiensis Soc^{is}
Jesu. 1628.—di Georgio Pernicelli. Ex dono Domini Bartholomei
Pernicelli.' Earl of Crawford (1887), no. 293.

Hain *2825. Proctor 6121. Huth I. 133.

149. ALBERTIS (LEO BAPTISTA DE). De re aedificatoria.
29 December 1485. F°.

Editio princeps. Prefatory letter by Angelo Poliziano to Lorenzo dei Medici.
Description in Hain (not as variant in Copinger).

Collation. a⁸ (a 1 not signed) b–d⁸ e⁶ f–o⁸ p⁷ q–z, & 9, Ɋ ⁸.

271 × 193 mm. Not rubricated. Numerous notes and careful architectural
drawings (c. 1500) in the margin.

Binding. Brown morocco of the eighteenth century, with the crest of
William Gulston, Bp of Bristol (†1684) on the back.
Provenance. Bp Gulston †1684. 'White's sale' (Wodhull's handwriting).
Wodhull, 1886.
HC. *419. Proctor 6131.

ANTONIO MISCOMINI (1481)

150. AUGUSTINUS. La citta di Dio. [Not after 1483.] F°.
First Italian translation.
Description in Hain.
Collation. a^{12}, a–z, A–G^{10} H^{12}. First and last leaves (blank ?) gone.
265 × 190 mm. Not rubricated. In the first quire four different water-
marks occur.
Binding. Dark red grained morocco with gold and blind tooling (c. 1801).
Provenance. Bought of Thorpe in 1824. Syston Park 1884. Sotheby's
24 Nov. 1897, no. 834.
HC. *2071. Proctor 6145.

BARTOLOMMEO DI LIBRI (1482)

151. SAVONAROLA. Trattato contra gli astrologi. [Ab.
1490.] 4°.
Description in Hain, Copinger.
Collation. a^8 (qu. a 1 title in facsimile, a 2 marked 'a 3' text), bc^8 d^{10}.
Audin wrongly gives a^{10}. Two leaves at end, described by Copinger, not
here.
202 × 138 mm.
Binding. Shabby quarter morocco, paper sides.
Provenance. MS. note on upper cover 'Ad usum Fr. M. A. Costello (XIX
Cent.).' J. and J. Leighton (1905), no. 4631.
HC. 14378. Proctor 6274. Audin 6.

FRANCESCO BUONACCORSI (1485)

152. JACOPONE DA TODI. Laude. 28 September 1490. 4°.
Description in Hain.
Collation. A^8, a–q^8 r^6.
185 × 125 mm. The cut on sig. A 8*b* is of the author kneeling in adoration
before a vision of the Virgin and Child in a mandorla. Not rubricated.
Binding. Modern green morocco by M. Lortic. Gilt edges. Arms of the
Duc de Rivoli, Prince d'Essling, on side, and monogram of VM (qu.
M.V. ?) on back.
Provenance. See binding. J. and J. Leighton.
HC. 9355. Proctor 6310.

LORENZO DI FRANCESCO DI ALOPA (1492)

153. ANTHOLOGIA GRAECA. 1494. 4°.

Editio princeps.
Description in Hain, Morgan.
Collation. A–Ω, AA–KK, [ΛΛ]⁸; 280 leaves.
224×158 mm. Printed in capital letters. Not rubricated.
Binding. White vellum (saec. XVIII), with two lettering-pieces red and green leather.
Provenance. Payne and Foss, 1827. Bookplate of Comte D. Boutourlin (1839)¹, and E. H. Bunbury (1895).
HC. *1145. Proctor 6406. Morgan II. 137 (no. 416).

154. APOLLONIUS RHODIUS. Argonautica. 1496. 4°.

Editio princeps.
Description in Hain.
Collation. α–φ⁸ χ⁴; 172 leaves. Last leaf (blank?) gone.
227×161 mm. In capital letters. Not rubricated.
Binding. Mottled calf gilt (saec. XVIII).
Provenance. On the first leaf the signature 'Pauli Terhaarij Amstelodamæi.' 'Jam vero...Joannis Woerdani...Ultrajecti. 5 Maij 1651' and 'D. of Grafton 1781.' On the flyleaf 'Coll: per: H: Drury: Harroviae. 1815.' Drury sale (1827), no. 257.
HC. *1292. Proctor 6407.

TREVISO

BERNARD OF COLOGNE (1477)

155. MAIUS (JUNIANUS). De priscorum proprietate verborum. 1477. F°.

Ed. 2.
Description in Hain, Morgan.
Collation. a–c¹⁰, d–f⁸, g–r¹⁰, f⁸, s–x¹⁰·⁸ y¹⁰, aa¹², bb–ll¹⁰. 330 leaves.
322×220 mm. On the second leaf a rich blue initial letter (German) on a gold ground, with coloured marginal border.
Binding. Half-calf (saec. XVIII).
Provenance. The name of an earlier owner, of the year 1686, erased on the verso of the first leaf. Cholmley (1902) no. 761.
Hain *10540. Proctor 6483. Morgan II. 157 (no. 444).

---

¹ His books were offered for sale in Paris in 1839. For him and his library see G. W. Greene, _Historical Studies_ (1850) pp. 313–8. Cf. Brunet III. 1103 a.

VERONA

JOHANNES OF VERONA (1472)

156. VALTURIUS (ROBERTUS). De re militari. 1472. F⁰.

Editio princeps.
Description in Hain (262 leaves), Morgan (wrongly 264 leaves).
Collation. [aa⁶ a–g¹⁰ h¹⁴ i¹² kl¹⁰ m¹² n⁸ o⁶ p–r¹⁰ s¹² t–z, A¹⁰ B¹².]
335×225 mm. Fine gold initial letters with white vine ornamentation, the
first one with long marginal scroll. The three-line initial letters are
parti-coloured. Smaller initials in red or blue. Chapter headings in MS.
red, blue and pink alternating letters, or plain script. Fol. 7 repaired.
Large woodcuts by Francesco di Georgio or Matteo Pasti. These are
said to be the earliest woodcuts in any dated Italian book. (Cf.
Lippmann, *Wood engraving*, pp. 57–59.)
The only book issued by this printer under this name (cf. Morgan).
Binding. Modern brown morocco, with blind tooling.
Provenance. Alfred Higgins, F.S.A. (1904), lot 238, with bookplate.
For another copy see Appendix no. 317.
HC. *15847. Proctor 6912. Morgan II. 177 (no. 470).

BRESCIA

BONINUS DE BONINIS (1483)

157. GELLIUS (AULUS). Noctes Atticae. 3 March 1485. F⁰.

Fifth edition. 'Correctore Marco Scaramucino de Palatiolo.'
Description in Hain.
Collation. AA, BB, a⁸, b–d⁶ e⁸ f–o⁶ p⁸ q–z, &, ↄ ⁊, A⁶ B⁸.
302×201 mm. Not rubricated.
Binding. Modern purple morocco, gilt edges.
Provenance. Syston Park (1884) no. 210, with bookplates.
Notes have been washed out, and the paper in places has perished.
HC. *7521. Proctor 6958. L. Lechi, 35.

158. DANTE. La Divina Comedia col commento di Cristoforo
Landino. 31 May 1487. F⁰.

The first edition containing woodcuts.
Description in Hain, Copinger, Koch.
Collation. &⁸ a–i⁸ k⁶ l–r, aa–mm⁸ nn⁴, A⁶ B⁸ C–L⁶ (last leaf gone, blank?).

366 × 245 mm. The large gold initial letter on the first page of the text
rests on a blue panel decorated with flowers, and the surrounding scroll-
work occupies nearly two margins. At the foot of the page are the
arms of the original owner (Per pale dancetté, not coloured) within a
circular wreath and subscribed 'F M' in ink. Ordinary initials in plain
blue or red.

Woodcuts. For a reproduction of one see Essling.

Binding. Red morocco (saec. XIX).

Provenance. See above. Sir Thomas David Gibson Carmichael (1903)
with bookplate.

Another copy. See Appendix no. 319.

HC. 5948. Proctor 6973. Cf. Essling 531. Koch I. 5. Colomb de Batines
I. 49–52. L. Lechi, 43. F. Lippmann, 87. Reichling II. 161.

VICENZA

GIOVANNI OF RENO WITH D. BERTOCHUS (1481)

159. CATULLUS, TIBULLUS, PROPERTIUS; cum Statii Ṣylvis.
1481. F°.

Ed. 2.

Description in Hain.

Collation. ab⁸ c–e⁶ f–h⁸ i–l⁶ m⁸ no⁶ p⁸ q (7 leaves) r–t⁶ ux⁸. Cf. Brunet for
additional leaves containing 'Carmen Joannis Calphurnii.'

300 × 186 mm. Initial letters in plain blue. The first page of the text
'richly illuminated in the Florentine style, with blank shield in circular
wreath at foot.

Binding. Pink morocco with gold tooling (eighteenth century).

Provenance. Sunderland sale (1881), no. 2560.

HC. *4760. Proctor 7151. Brunet (1860) I. 1676–7.

HERMANN LICHTENSTEIN (1478)

160. OVIDIUS. Opera. 10 May, 12 August 1480. F°.

With dedicatory epistle by Bonus Accursius to Ciccho Simoneta. This
edition was edited by Barnaba Celsano of Vicenza.

Description in Hain.

Collation. a¹⁰ b–z, aa–hh⁸ (last leaf gone, blank?); [ ]⁶ (first leaf gone,
blank?) A¹⁰ B–V⁸ (v⁸ gone, blank?).

282 × 192 mm. Not rubricated. Some MS. notes (saec. XV–XVI).
Binding. Paper boards (in two volumes).
Provenance. Not recorded.
HC. *12141. Proctor 7157.

RIGO DI CA ZENO (1480)
(HENRICUS DE S. URSO)

161. CAPELLA (MARTIANUS). Opera. 16 December 1499. Fº.

Editio princeps. Dedicatory epistle of 'Franciscus Vitalis Bodianus' to
 Giovanni Chaeregti (Johannes de Chaeregato), bishop of Cattaro.
Description in Hain.
Collation. ab⁸ c–u⁶ (last gone, blank ?). Not rubricated.
315 × 210 mm.
Binding. Brown calf.
Provenance. From the University of Ferrara, with stamp.
Hain *4370. Proctor 7174.

UNKNOWN PLACE AND PRINTER

[FLORENCE ?]

162. PHALARIS. Epistole. 1471. 4º.

First edition of the Italian translation by Bartolomeo Fontio.
Description in Hain, Morgan.
Collation. [a–d¹⁰ e–g⁸.] 64 leaves.
213 × 150 mm. Initials in plain red.
Binding. Russia.
Provenance. Bought of Boone. Initials 'E.C.L. 1865.' Bookplate of
 Edward Cheney (1886). Gennadius (1895).
Hain *12903. Proctor 7347. Morgan II. 121 (no. 396).

SWITZERLAND

BASLE

BERTHOLD RUPPEL (1468)

163. CONRADUS DE MURE. Repertorium vocabulorum exquisitorum oratorie poesis et historiarum. [1468?] F°.

Description in Hain.
Collation. [a–d¹⁰ e¹² f–n¹⁰ op⁸.] Last leaf gone, blank?
282 × 205 mm. Finely rubricated throughout, with red or blue initials. Much water-stained and mended in places.
Binding. Pigskin with metal corner and centre pieces and red label (XIX cent.).
Provenance. On the first and last page of the book occurs the inscription : 'Collegii Epi*scop*alis Vien*nensis* ad S. Nicolaum.'
Hain *11642. Proctor 7448.

MICHAEL WENSSLER (1474) WITH FRIEDRICH BIEL

164. BARZIZIUS (GASPARINUS). Epistolae. [1475?] F°.

Description in Hain.
Collation. [a–f¹⁰.] 60 leaves.
280 × 200 mm. Not rubricated.
Binding. Red morocco with gold tooling and gilt edges (eighteenth century).
Provenance. Firmin Didot and Morante (1872) bookplates.
Hain *2675. Proctor 7466.

165. CLEMENS V. Constitutiones cum apparatu domini Joannis Andreae. 2 May 1476. F°.

Description in Hain.
Collation. [a–e¹⁰ f–h⁸.] 74 leaves.
398 × 285 mm. The large initial letter on the first leaf parti-coloured in blue, black, and red. Ordinary initials and paragraph marks in blue or red. Text capitals touched in red.

Binding. Cerise calf binding with plain gold tooling, by Tout.
Provenance. Henry White (1902) no. 537.
Hain *5419. Proctor 7478.

JOHANN OF AMORBACH (1478)

166. SCOTT (MICHAEL). Liber phisionomie magistri Michaelis
Scoti. [Ab. 1486.] 4°.
Description in Hain.
Collation. a–e⁸; 40 leaves.
201 × 135 mm. Not rubricated.
Binding. Speckled brown calf, with Greek key-pattern border. Red edges.
Provenance. R. B. Stewart (1888) with bookplate.
Hain *14545 = *14551. Proctor 7617.

JOHANN BERGMANN DE OLPE (1494)

167. BRANT (SEBASTIAN). Stultifera Navis. 1 March 1498. 4°.
Fifth Latin edition.
Description in Hain, Morgan.
Collation. a–s⁸, ſ, t–y⁴. Last leaf gone, blank?
217 × 155 mm. Not rubricated. 117 woodcuts and device. The mark of
type sideways, by accident, in the middle of the woodcut on fol. LXXVIII a.
Binding. Limp vellum.
Provenance. J. and J. Leighton (1905 catalogue), no. 627.
Hain *3751. Proctor 7778. Morgan I. 244 (no. 235).

168. REUCHLIN.(JOHANN). Scenica Progymnasmata. 1498. 4°.
Editio princeps. Cf. no. 189.
Description in Hain-Copinger (collation wrong). Three bars of printed
music in the text.
Collation. a⁸ b⁴; 12 leaves.
200 × 138 mm. Not rubricated.
'Reuchlin has translated, or rather imitated Blanchet's admirable farce of
Pathelin. See Warton *Hist. Poet.* ii. 375 where however there are some
mistakes which I have corrected. See Hist. de la littérature allemande
1781, 12° p. 39; Bibliothèque of Du Verdier ed. Juvigny v. 378.'
(Notes from F. Douce's copy in the Bodleian Library, with additions by
W. E. Buckley, inserted here.)
Binding. Half red roan, red paper sides.
Provenance. W. E. Buckley (1893). J. and J. Leighton (1905 catalogue),
no. 4375.
HC. 13882 (incorrect). Proctor 7781.

FRANCE

PARIS

GEORG WOLF AND JOHANN PHILIPPI
(1494)

169. BECKET (THOMAS). Vita et processus sancti Thome Cantuariensis martyris super libertate ecclesiastica. 27 March 1495–6. 4°.

> The only edition of this book printed in the fifteenth century.
> *Description* in Copinger.
> *Collation.* a–l⁸ m⁶ A⁴. Part of no. 170, as the signatures indicate.
> 222 × 156 mm. Not rubricated.
> *Binding.* Whole red grained morocco and gilt edges by H. Faulkner, London, with label. Bound with no. 170.
> *Provenance.* With MS. inscriptions 'Bibliothecae Colbertinae' (1728) and 'J. Milners.' Henry White (1902) with bookplate.
> HC. 15510. Proctor 8238. Chawner 157.

170. BERTRANDUS (PETRUS), Cardinalis. Liber contra Petrum de Cugneriis. 2 April 1495. 4°.

> *Description* in Hain.
> *Collation.* aa⁸ bb¹⁰; 18 leaves. Part of no. 169, as the signatures indicate.
> 222 × 156 mm. Not rubricated.
> *Binding.* See no. 169.
> *Provenance.* With no. 169.
> HC. 3002. Proctor 8239. Chawner 158. Pellechet 2251.

JEAN MAURAND (1493)

171. CHRONIQUES DE FRANCE. 30 August 1493. F°.

> Known as the 'Chroniques de Saint Denis.' Printed for A. Verard.
> Vol. III. only.
> *Description* in Copinger.

S. C.   5

Collation. AAA⁸ (1 and 8 gone), AAA⁸, BBB⁸ (1 and 8 gone), CCC–FFF⁸, GGG⁸ (leaf 5 gone), HHH–QQQ⁸, RRR⁶, SSS⁸ (leaf 4 gone), TTT–XXX, AAAA–KKKK⁸, LLLL⁶, MMMM⁶ (last gone, blank?).

360 × 255 mm.   Rubricated.   Woodcuts.

Binding. Old leather with gilt corners, about 1550, very much tattered.

Provenance. On the first leaf of the text the blank shield at foot is filled in by pen with an ecclesiastical coat of arms.

On the last leaf pen-trials and notes.

HC. 5008. Proctor 8291. Pellechet 3576. Cf. Claudin *Histoire de l'imprimerie en France*, II. 451–6.

LYONS

JOHANN SIBER (1489)

172. GUIDO DE BAYSIO. Rosarium decretorum. [Ab. 1498?] Large F⁰.

Description in Hain.

Collation in Copinger.

386 × 273 mm.   Two leaves only, sig. f ii, f iii, inserted as fly-leaves in no. 89.

Provenance. Not recorded.

HC. *2714. Proctor 8551.

HOLLAND

UTRECHT

NICOLAAS KETELAER AND GERARDUS LEEMPT (1473)

173. KEMPIS (THOMAS À). Tractatus varii. [1473–4.] Fᵒ.

Editio princeps.

Description in HC., Campbell.

Collation [a⁸ b–i¹⁰ kl⁶ m⁸ no¹⁰ pq⁸ r–x¹⁰ y⁸ z¹⁰ &⁸].

280×203 mm. Rubricated.

Binding. Original wooden boards covered with stamped leather, stamped with 'b.d.,' 'Ihesus,' 'Maria,' 'IHS' medallion, rosette, fleur-de-lis, and the pelican in her piety. Metal clasps. Rebacked.

Provenance. Inside the front cover and on the first flyleaf occur the three following inscriptions (1) 'Liber marie castri prope dulmaniam,' (2) 'Dyt bueck hoert to marien flot by dulman,' (3) 'Pertinet domui castri marie prope Dulmaniam ordinis Carthusiensis.'

HC. 9768. Campbell *Annales* *1657. Proctor 8849.

JAN VELDENER (1478)

174. ROLEWINCK (W.). Cronijcken van Ouden Tijden. 14 February 1480. Fᵒ.

This is the Dutch version of the Fasciculus Temporum, of which Veldener had already printed the Latin at Louvain in 1475; but the present book contains nearly twice as much matter as the Latin. The oldest printed armorial, containing 248 escutcheons.

Thirty-four woodcuts of towns and persons (Cockerell). On fol. 2 are a handsome woodcut border and initial. The border is repeated on fol. 9.

Description in HC., Campbell, and Morgan.

Collation (as in Morgan) [A, a–z, &, aa–dd⁸, ee⁶, ff⁸, gg⁴, hh–ss⁸]. 338 leaves. Folio 'clxxxv' missed in foliation, and 'CClviij' duplicated.

273×205 mm. The decorative border cut into.

The book is rubricated, and very carefully and artistically coloured throughout.

Binding. Old calf binding with stamped border (sixteenth century).
Provenance. Inscription on fly-leaf, 'Ex libris Petri Theodori van Thuijne' (XVII cent.). Bought of Quaritch in 1904 (Cat. 229, no. 764).
HC. 6946. CA. *1479. Proctor 8858. Conway, p. 325. Chawner 172. Morgan III. 99 (no. 626). S. C. Cockerell, *Woodcuts*, p. 34.

GOUDA

GERARDUS LEEU (1477)

175. DIALOGUS CREATURARUM MORALIZATUS. 3 June 1480. F°.

First edition. For the second edition see Appendix no. 330.
Description in Campbell, Morgan.
Collation in Morgan. [aa⁴ bb⁶] a–l⁸, m⁶; 104 leaves.
Wants leaves 1 and 11, and sig. g 8.
247 × 185 mm. The extremely handsome border of the twelfth leaf (first leaf of text) is cut into on all three sides, and leaves 1 and 11 (both blank) gone. Initial letters, paragraph marks in plain red or blue. Initial strokes in yellow. The painted letter 'Q' on the second leaf particoloured in red and blue, filled in with red diaper work and blue streamers. Fol. 12 is coloured in delicate yellow, green, and pink and the woodcut S has 'Ihesus Maria' inserted by hand in blue. The 123 cuts of the book and the printer's mark are all coloured in the same manner.
Binding. Blue grained morocco with gold tooling and gilt edges.
Provenance. On the second leaf are the inscriptions 'Capucinorum Leodiensium.' J. and J. Leighton.
Hain 6124. CA. *560. Proctor 8920. Conway, p. 329. Morgan III. 121 (no. 644).

ZWOLLE

PIETER VAN OS (1479)

First Press

176. GREGORIUS I. De cura pastorali. 1480. 4°.
Description in Campbell.
Collation. a⁸ (leaves 3 and 4 marked a 1, 2), b–p⁸. 120 leaves.
206 × 135 mm. Plain rubrication.
Binding. With no. 37
Provenance. Ibid.
HC. 7984. CA. 856 (*for* piij *read* piiij).

BELGIUM

LOUVAIN

JOHN OF PADERBORN (1474)
'Johannes de Westphalia'

177. CRESCENTIIS (PETRUS DE). Liber ruralium commodorum.
9 December 1474. F⁰.

> John of Paderborn's first dated book. The second edition of this work.
> *Description* in Hain, Campbell, Morgan.
> *Collation* (in Morgan) [a–i^{10} k^{12} l–t^{10} v^6]. 198 leaves. First and last, blank, gone.
> 264 × 190 mm. Carefully rubricated with plain red initial letters.
> *Binding.* Brown marbled calf with gold back, and arms of Gaspar Joseph de Servais, 1755–1807, of Mechlin, on the sides. See B. Linnig, *Bibliothèques*, 1906, p. 123. Bound by Derome le jeune, with his label.
> *Provenance.* See above.
> HC. *5829. CA. *501. Proctor 9208. Morgan II. 100 (no. 627).

ANTWERP

GERARDUS LEEU (1484)

178. LUDOLPHUS DE SAXONIA. Leven ons Heeren Ihesu Christi. 3 November 1487. 4⁰.

> The first edition of the translation into Dutch.
> *Description* in Campbell, Morgan.
> *Collation.* ab^8 c–f^6 g^8 h–z, and, 9, A–L, aa–oo^6. 306 leaves. Folios 301, 305, and 306 in facsimile.
> 256 × 181 mm. Rubricated. With printed initial letters; and woodcuts, fairly coloured.
> *Binding.* Blue morocco, with gold centrepiece by Rivière and Son.
> *Provenance.* Charles Lilburn (bookplate).
> CA. *1181. Proctor 9369. Conway, p. 332. Morgan II. 129 (no. 651).

SPAIN

VALENCIA

LAMBERT PALMART

179. PEREZ (JACOBUS) de Valentia. Expositio in canticum canticorum. 19 May 1486. F⁰.

Description [six leaves not seen] [sig. a 1]. Prologus. // ( )Antabo dilecto // meo canticuz vi // nee sue. ysa. v. Li // ... [a 8 col. 2]. Incipit // ergo canticum primum. // ( )Sculetur me os // culo oris sui. [o 8 b. Colophon as in Haebler *Bibl.*] No copy recorded as above.

Collation [A⁶ not seen], a–m⁸ n⁶ o⁸.

302 × 210 mm. Without rubrication.

Binding. Modern crimson morocco, with antique blind tooling by J. and J. Leighton.

Provenance. No marks of ownership.

Cf. Hain 12592. Cf. Proctor 9499. Cf. Haebler, *Bibliografía*, p. 255; *Early Printers*, p. 91, pl. XXIX.

SARAGOSSA

MATTHEW OF FLANDERS

OR

PAUL HURUS

180. RODRIGO DE ZAMORA. Espejo de la vida humana. 13 May 1491. F⁰.

Description in Haebler.

Collation. a–o⁸ pq⁶. This copy wants a 1 and i 7 to the end (fifty-five leaves). A pen copy of the last leaf inserted.

280 × 210 mm. Woodcut initial letters. Fine powerful woodcuts nearly the width of the page, surrounded by border pieces, on which see Haebler. Several cuts appear to be identical with those used in Zainer's Augsburg edition of 1475, afterwards used at Lyons, as pointed out to me by Mr Cockerell. A few pen-marks.

Binding. Eighteenth century light brown calf.

Provenance. Not recorded.

Hain 13954. Haebler, *Early Printers*, pp. 92 and 113; *Bibliografia*, pp. 277–8. Cf. S. C. Cockerell, *German Woodcuts*, no. 12–14.

SEVILLE

PIERRE BRUN AND GIOVANNI GENTILE

181. MEJIA (HERNANDO). Libro de la Nobleza. 30 June 1492. F°.

Description in Haebler *Bibl.* (very incorrect), Morgan.

Collation. a⁶ b–h⁸ i¹⁰ k–m⁸.

284 × 215 mm. Woodcut initials (see Haebler). The text title on sig. a 5 and b 1 printed in red. Numerous pen-marks. Several heraldic woodcuts, rudely engraved, on three of the last four leaves.

Binding. Modern crimson morocco with blind tooling in antique style by J. and J. Leighton.

Provenance. On the half-title three names of previous owners obliterated.

HC. 11133. Proctor 9545. Haebler, *Bibliografia*, p. 195 (no. 411), *Early Printers*, p. 96 (and plate xx^a). Morgan III. 149 (no. 666).

THE SIXTEENTH CENTURY ETC.

GERMANY

AUGSBURG

182. BAYER (JOHANN). Uranometria...nova methodo delineata. Christophorus Mangus, Augustae Vindelicorum. 1603. Fº.

Star-atlas engraved on metal by Alexander Mair.

Collation. 1 (title), a 1, b², A–Z, Aa–Zz, Aaa–Ccc².

368 mm.

Binding. Original brown calf, with gold tooling. Metal clasps and corner pieces.

Provenance. This copy was presented by Nicholas Vicke to the Library at Breslau, and bears on the verso of the title the following inscription:

> "Per angusta ad augusta
> Sic per Oppositum nascitur omne Bonum.

Sacratissimae Caesareae, nec non in Ungaria et Bohemia Regiae Mtis Domini mei Clementissimi DAPIFER, et Serenissimi SUECORUM Gothorum Vandalorumque Electi Regis CAROLI Consiliarius et Commissarius Bellicus Supremus NICOLAUS VICKE, Nobilium et Spectabilium Dominorum Vratislauiensium Bibliothecam hoc libro Astronomico in perpetuam sui memoriam exornare uoluit, Anno Salutis M.DC.IIII., die 25 Februarij."

Library mark copy: 'Ex Bibl. ad aed. Mar. Magdal.' A. Cowper Ranyard (1895). W. Wesley and Son, booksellers, London.

A. G. Kästner, *Gesch.* IV. 95. Graesse i. 314. Alg. Deutsch. Biog. ii. 188.

FRANKFORT

183. BRY (THEODOR DE). America. [Grands Voyages. Latin. Part IV.] 1594. F°.

First edition: second issue. Title and 24 plates only, without the text.
Title. Americae pars quarta *etc.*
The imprint reads Rudolph (*see* Lord Crawford), but there is no AZ at the lower right-hand corner.
Plate II is of the variety with the 'pavillon' of three fleurs de lis on the mizen-mast (*see* Crawford *note*).
Binding. Half-vellum.
Provenance. Quaritch.
BM. Brunet I. 1327. Lord Crawford, *Bibliotheca Lindesiana: Collations and Notes*, no. 3 (London, 1884), pp. 129–131.

184. DE BRY (J. THEODOR and J. I.). India. [Petits Voyages. Latin. Part V.] M. Becker. 1601. Small F°.

Plates only, with their title. The plates delicately coloured.
Collation. a⁴ b⁴ c–e⁴ [f²], last leaf blank, gone; 21 leaves only.
Binding. Modern olive half morocco.
Provenance. C. Serrure (1873). Ant. van Bellingen, Antwerp, 1873, as no. 185.
Brunet I. 1337. Lord Crawford, p. 171.

185. DE BRY (J. T. and J. I.). India. [Petits Voyages. Latin. Part VI.] Icones. W. Richter. Small F°. 1603.

Plates only, with their title. Coloured.
Collation. A–G⁴; 28 leaves, last leaf blank, wanting in this copy.
Plates II and III with the texts in the reverse order (see Brunet and Crawford). Note that in some editions Plate XXV has been re-engraved, a fact which, it would appear, has not been previously remarked. In the present copy there is no strong line enclosing the picture, the two animals at the base are standing upon nothing, and nine sailing ships are represented. In the copy in the Cambridge University Library there is a strong external line, the animals stand on ground, and there are eight ships only: the whole plate is coarser and apparently later.
Binding. Modern olive half morocco.
Provenance. Same as no. 184.
Brunet i. 1338. Lord Crawford, p. 173.

186. DE BRY (J. T. and J. I.). India. [Petits Voyages. Latin. Part VII.] Icones. W. Richter. 1606. Small F^o.

Plates X–XXII only. Delicately coloured. The plates have Roman numerals. Engraver's mark IG on plate XII, but not dated (see Crawford). *Binding.* Half-cloth. *Provenance.* Not recorded. Brunet i. 1339. Lord Crawford, p. 175.

INGOLSTADT

187. APIANUS (PETRUS)[1]. Quadrans Astronomicus. In officina Apiani, 6 July 1532. Small F^o.

Title. ꝫꝭ QUADRANS APIANI ꙮꙮ ASTRONOMICUS ET IAM RECENS INVENTUS ET NVNC PRIMVM EDITUS. Huic adiuncta sunt & alia instrumenta obseruatoria perinde noua, adcommodata horis discernendis nocturnis simul & diurnis, idꝗ ex Sole, Luna, Stellisꝗ tum erraticis cum fixis, ad quoꝶ tamen cognitionem cuiꝗ citra omnem Preceptoris operam facile peruenire licebit. Deinde altitudinis etiam, distantiæ, profunditatisꝗ Puteorum, Turriumꝗ seu ædificiorum adnexæ sunt dimensiones, & aquarum quoꝗ ex monte vno in alium deductiones. His omnibus accedit, quo pacto per speculum altitudines structurarum uarijs modis cognosci queant. Et quomodo extensis noctu digitis (naturali quodam, quod & Diogenes admiraretur, instrumento) siugulæ [*sic*] horæ noctis obseruari commode possint. [Cut of quadrant.] Cum Gratia & Priuilegio Cæsareo, cuius exemplar adiectum est Astronomico Imperatorio, quod iā recens edidimus. Anno M.D.XXXII.

Collation. A–E⁴ F² G⁴; twenty-six leaves. *Description.* A1 *a*, Title. A1 *b*, blank. A2 *a*, Dedication. A2 *b*, Verses. A3 *a*–G4 *a*, Text, with forty-eight cuts. G4 *a*, Errata and colophon. G4 *b*, blank. Not bound. Contemporary marginal notes. *Provenance.* No. 2047 in some catalogue.

188. APIANUS (PETRUS). Astronomicon Caesareum. 1540. Large F^o.

[A1] Astronomicum Cæsareum. [Col. sig. O5b] Factum et actum Ingolstadii in aedibus nostris. Anno a christo nato sesquimillesimo quadragesimo mense maio (*see note*). [O6a] Insignia Petri Apiani, Mathemat. Ingolstadien.

---

[1] Bienewitz.

A–F⁴, G⁴+1, H–N⁴ O⁶. Movable discs affixed with silk on B3, C1 (silk), C3 (four discs), C4 (silk), D1 (six), D2 (silk), D3 (four), D4 (silk), E1 (two), E2 (six), E3 (silk), E4 (eight), F1 (silk), F2 (seven), F3 (two), F4 (two), G1 (silk), G2 (silk), G3b (five), G4 (three), G5 (three), H1 (silk), J2 (silk), K3 (four), K4 (three), L1 (three), L2 (one), L3 (one), L4 (two), M1 (two), M3 (two), M4 (silk).   On sig. B3 one movable disc only, with zodiacal signs (see Brunet).

The whole book beautifully coloured, and in places gilded.

On the penultimate leaf the colophon is printed with type cast in reverse.

This book is referred to in a letter from Dr Nicholas Wotton to King Henry the Eighth, written at Speier on 11 June 1544:

> Petrus Appianus, 'a man of great name in the arts mathematicals,' has shown Wotton that, hearing of Henry's learning and delight in liberal sciences, he meant to present a book of his own, named *Astronomicum Cesareum*, containing divers new things. He has printed it himself, as he does all his books, and not above sixteen or seventeen copies, and, albeit it is dedicated to the Emperor and his brother, he would send it because otherwise Henry could not come by it. This Apianus is the ordinary reader of the 'mathematicalles' in the Unyversitie of Ingolstadt, and is very familiar with the Fowkers, through whose agent in England an answer may be sent him. (*Letters and Papers Foreign and Domestic, of the reign of Henry the VIII.* Arr. by J. Gairdner and R. H. Brodie. Vol. XIX, Part I, 1903, no. 677.)

Binding. Half-calf, paper sides.

Provenance. Armorial bookplate of Count Nostitz von Rokitnitz (see Rietstap, II. 327), with initials 'C. W. G. V. N.' Signatures of 'Oswaldi de Egkh' and 'Jean Bernard Comte d'Herberstein.'

Brunet I. 342. Delambre, *Histoire de L'Astronomie du Moyen Age,* Paris, 1819, pp. 390–397; K. Falkenstein, *Beschreibung der k. öff. Bibliothek zu Dresden,* 1839, pp. 791–2; Graesse, i. 160. Houzeau et Lancaster. For the author see *A.D.B.* I. 506, and for the book and author Didot, *Nouv. Biog. Univ.* (a long quotation from Delambre).

PFORZHEIM

THOMAS ANSHELM

189.   REUCHLIN (JOHANN). Scenica Progymnasmata. 1509. 4°.

Collation. ab⁶; 12 leaves. With four lines of music (cf. no. 168).

The margins covered with annotations in red and black ink (saec. XVI).

Binding. Half red morocco, by Birdsall and Son.

Provenance. J. and J. Leighton.

Brunet IV. 1254. Panzer VIII. 231. 31.

STRASSBURG

J. GRÜNINGER

190. BOETHIUS. De consolatione Philosophiae. 24 August 1501. F⁰.

Woodcuts and initial letters.
264·5 mm.
Binding. Vellum.
Provenance. W. H. Crawford of Lakelands (1891) no. 400, with bookplate.

191. ——. Another copy.

278 mm.
Wants first six leaves.
Binding. Half-vellum.
Provenance. Rev. Walter Sneyd (1903), lot 112, with bookplate.
Brunet I. 1034. Proctor 9886. Muther 555.

192. VERGILIUS. Opera. 27 August 1502. Small F⁰.

Title. Publij Virgilij marōis opera. [Cut.]
301 × 205 mm. With cuts.
Binding. Brown calf with blind tooling and blue edges.
Provenance. A. Firmin Didot (1867), no. 157.
Brunet V. 1277. Proctor 9888. Muther 557.

193. GEILER (JOHANN). Doctor Keiserspegrs (*sic*). Passion· Des Herē Jesu. 1513. Small F⁰

German translation by Johannes Adelphus, i.e. J. A. Mülich.
Cuts and initial letters. Ff. cxii. For the cuts see Muther.
Binding. Red morocco, gilt edges (Capé).
Provenance. MS. inscription on title: '1513. Wer hillfft mir C. V. Winizeeren.'
BM. Muther 1433.

JOHANN KNOBLOUCH

194. GREGORIUS NAZIANZENUS. Libelli decem. 13 Jan. 1508. 4⁰.

Description. [a 1] Hi sunt in hoc Codice libelli | X. diui Gregorij Nazanzeni...[a 2].
Preface by Joannes Adelphus Mulingus (i.e. J. A. Mülich) to Georgius Bohem and Joannes Flamingus. [b1 *a*] Incipit prefatō Rufini. [b1 *b*] Text. [Col.] Explicit liber...translatus a quodā Rufino...M.d.viij. Hilarij. [Printer's mark.]

168 mm.   Not rubricated.   A few marginal notes (saec. XVI).
Binding.   Green paper boards.
Provenance.   Not recorded.
Panzer VI. 41. 120.   Proctor 10059.

195. GELDENHAUR (GERARDUS) NOVIOMAGUS.   De terrifico
Cometa.   1527.   4°.

Description (Title).   De terrifico Cometa, cui à condito orbe similis uisus
   non est, qui ap-|paruit Anno M.D.XXVII. mense Octobri, Epistola ad
   Ca|rolum V. Impe.. Cæs. August. P. F. Victorem Gall. Pont. P. P.   [Full
   page woodcut partly printed in red.]
Dedication to the emperor on the second leaf, in which the author states
   that he had the account of it from Petrus Creusser, the astrologer.   This
   work does not appear in the account of the author in *Allgemeine Deutsche
   Biographie.*
Collation.   A⁴ B² (last leaf blank); six leaves.
195 mm.
Binding.   Modern brown calf.
Provenance.   H. W. Cholmley (1902) no. 695.
Panzer IX. 146, 391 b.

ITALY

FLORENCE

196. PETRARCA. Canzoniere et Triomphi. Philippo di Giunta. April 1515. 8º.

The title in an architectural compartment. Cuts.

154 mm.

Binding. Half russia, paper sides.

Provenance. On the last page are various pen-trials : 'Dotto...Corrado principe di Salerno Bergnon.' 'Giulio Gonzaga.' 'Alla Illma donna Isabella Gonzaga.' J. and J. Leighton (1905), no. 3945.

Brunet IV. 546. Renouard 64.

197. BOCCACCIO. Laberinto d' amore. B. di Giunta. 1525. 8º

Description (Title). LABERINTO D' AMORE DI M. GIO-|VANNI BOCCACCIO CON | una Epistola à Messer Pino de Ros|si confortatoria del me-|desimo autore. [Col.] Imp̄sso in Firenze nellāno del Signore .M.D.XXV.

After the title is the preface of Bernardo di Giunta 'a gli Amatori della Lingua Toscana' (2 pp.).

First printed in 1487, again in 1515 and 1516.

160 mm. Ff. 72. Not rubricated.

Binding. Black grained morocco, gilt. Silk lining.

Provenance. Not recorded.

Brunet I. 1016. Renouard 79.

198. BOCCACCIO. Ameto: Comedia. Heredi di P. de Giunta. 29 May 1529. 8º.

Description (Title). AMETO DEL BOCCACCIO. Dedication by Bernardi di Giunta to Giovanni Serristori (3 pp.). [Col.] Impreso in Firenze per gli heredi di Philippo de Giunta Nellanno...M.D.XXIX. adi. xxix. di Maggio. Sig. N7 and N8 a blank. N8 *b*, printer's device.

Ff. 104.

Binding. Modern white vellum.

Provenance. Not recorded.

Brunet I. 992. Renouard 103.

199. BOCCACCIO. Decameron. F. and J. Giunti, e fratelli. 1573. 4⁰.

Description (Title).

Il | Decameron | Di Messer | Giovanni Boccacci | Cittadino Fiorentino. | Ricorretto in Roma, et Emendato secondo | l' ordine del Sacro Conc. di Trento, | Et riscontrato in Firenze con Testi Antichi & alla sua | vera lezione ridotto da' Deputati di loro Alt. Ser. | Nuouamente Stampato. | Con Priuilegij del Sommo Pontefice, delle Maestadi del Re Christianissimo & | Re Cattolico, delli Serenissimi Gran Duca & Principe di Toscana, | dell' Ill. et Ecc. S. Duca di Ferrara, et d' altri Sign. et Rep. | [Printer's Mark.] | In Fiorenza | Nella Stamperia de i Giunti | MDLXXIII. | [Col.] In Fiorenza | Nella Stamperia di Filippo & | Iacopo Giunti, e' fratelli. | 1573.

217 mm. Pp. (32)+578+(4).

Binding. Old Italian vellum, gilt edges, green ties.

Provenance. Sale no. 291.

Brunet I. 1001.

PADUA

200. TASSO. La Gerusalemme Liberata. P. P. Tozzi. 1628. 4⁰.

Description (Title).

La Gerusalemme Liberata di Torquato Tasso Con la Vita di lui, Con gli Argomenti à ciascun Canto di Bartolomeo Barbato con le Annotationi di Scipio Gentile, e di Giulio Guastauini, e con le Notizie historiche di Lorenzo Pignoria. In Padoua Per Pietro Paolo Tozzi M.D.C.XXVIII.

232 mm. Pp. (16)+408. Illustration. Portrait signed D.H.F. and illustrations signed G. G. Franco (p. 276).

Extra-illustration, 'Giacomo Frāco,' and Bernardo Castello, from the Genoa edition of 1590. The plates are much worn.

Binding. Old Italian vellum.

Provenance. Signatures of 'Elizabetta dal Medico' and S. Gastinova.

Graesse VI. ii. 33.

PARMA

201. OVID. Metamorphoses. F. Mazalis. 1 May 1505. F⁰

With the commentary of Raphael Regius.

Description (Title). Habebis candide lector *etc.* [Col.] Impressum Parmæ Expensis & Labore Francisci Mazalis Calcographi diligentissimi. M.D.V. Cal. Maii.

With cuts (see Essling).

Binding. Plain vellum (saec. XVII).

Provenance. Not recorded.

Essling 226.

ROME

202. LAURO (GIACOMO). Antiquae Urbis splendor. G. Mascardi.
1612–1615. Oblong 4°.

Description. (Title):
Antiquae . Urbis Splendor Hoc . est . praecipua . eiusdem . templa . amphi-
theatra . theatra . circi . naumachiæ . arcus . triumphales...Opera & in-
dustria Iacobi Lauri Romani in æs incisa...Romae...MDCXII.
Three books. Book I, originally containing 42 leaves, wants fol. 5. Books
II and III consist of 44 leaves each.
Description. Vol. I. Title engraved, followed by (1) Antiquae Urbis.
(2) Vera Capitolii...topographia. (3) Dedication to Sigismund III.
(4) Missing. (5) Portrait of Sigismund III. 1609. (6) General Title
('Roma Vetus' &c,). (7) Three printed leaves: Iacobus Laurus Lec-
tori. (Imprint: Appresso Giacomo Mascardi. 1614.) Clemens Papa
VIII. 1598. (Imprint: Ex Typographia Reverendae Camerae Apos-
tolicae. 1614.) Matthias...Imperator. (Same imprint. 1614.) (8) 32
plates.
Vol. II. (1) Dedication to Charles Emanuel Duke of Savoy. (2) Antiqui-
tatum Urbis Liber Secundus. 1613. (3) Portrait of Charles Emanuel.
1613. (4) 41 plates follow.
Vol. III. (1) Engraved title: Antiquæ Urbis Splendoris Cōplementū. 1615.
(2) Printed Dedication to Ranucci Farnese, Duke of Parma. (3) Three
plates of Visio Danielis, Romani Imperii Imago, De Ponte et Porta
Triumphali in Vaticano. (4) Romanorum...triumphi. (5) (2 leaves
printed). 8 plates follow. (6) De terrestribus...copiis (1 page printed).
(7) 28 plates follow.
213 × 290 mm.
Binding. Olive morocco, gilt edges. In one volume.
Provenance. Sale no. 244.
Cf. Brunet III. 881.

TOSCOLANO

203. DANTE. Divina Comedia. [A. Paganini. About 1502
or 1527.] 8°.

Description. Title (in capitals). [ai] Dante col sito, et forma dell' inferno
[a1b] Lo 'nferno e 'l purgatorio e 'l paradiso di Dante Alaghieri. [Col.
qu. woodcut?] P. Alex. Pag. Benacenses. F. Bena. V. V.
Ff. (248). 3 diagrams at end. The last part of the inscription is said to
mean 'Fecerunt Benacenses. Viva. Viva,' and to record the establish-
ment of their printing office in Toscolano.

S. C.

6

Ab. 1502 (Colomb de Batines).   Ab. 1527 (Lechi).   *See* Brunet.
155 mm.
Binding.   Olive morocco, gilt edges, by J. Mackenzie.
Provenance. · Not recorded.
Koch I. 7.   Brunet II. 502.

VENICE

204.   DEMOSTHENES.   Orationes duæ et sexaginta: Libanii
argumenta: Vita Demosthenis per Libanium.   Ejusdem vita per
Plutarchum.   In aedibus Aldi, Mense Novem. 1504.   Fº.

Second edition.
Edited by Aldus and Scipio Carteromachus.   With autograph signature
'Camilli Lupi.'
280×179 mm.
Binding.   Maroon morocco, gilt tooled, and gilt edges, bound by Hayday.
Provenance.   Baron Seillière (1887), no. 353 with label.
Brunet II. 587.   D. Clement VIII. 144-7.   Renouard 477.

205.   EUCLIDES.   Elementorum Libri I–XIV, etc.   Interpr. B.
Zamberto.   Joh. Tacuinus.   25 Oct. 1505.   Fº.

[Fol. 1.   Euclidis Megarēsis philosophi...(gone).]   2—7 b Ad...Guidonem
Vrbini Ducem...B. Zamberti...Protheoria.   7 b—10 b Vita Euclidis, &c.
Castigationes.   10 b [ends] Ber. Cre. Compegit.   [Sig. A 1 with three-
quarter border] Euclidis...elemento*U* liber primus ex traditione Theonis
Bartholameo Zāberto Uene. interp̄te.   '[Sig. Y1 b ends] Euclidis...
Libri XIIII. Finis.   [Y2 a] Bartholomaeus...Paulo Pisano...foelicitatem
perpetuam.   [Y 2 b] Phaenomena.   [Z 6 b] Specularia.   [AA 5] Per-
spectiua.   [BB 8 b] Protheoria Marini, &c.   [CC 5] Liber Datorum ex
traditione Pappi...[FF 5 a ends]   ❡ Impressum Venetiis...in edibus
Iohannis Tacuini...M.D.V. VIII. Klendas (*sic*) nouēbris...[Last leaf blank
gone.]
299 × 198 mm.   Cuts and initial letters.
Binding. · Mottled calf.
Provenance.   Not recorded.
D. Clement VIII. 144-7 (full description).   Essling 283.   BM.   Cf. Brunet
II. 1088.

206.   OVIDIUS.   Heroides cum commentariis etc.   J. Tacuinus.
30 July 1510.   Fº.

Title.   Epistole Heroides...figuris ornate: cōmentātib⁹ Antonio Volsco &
Ubertino Cresentinate in Ibin vero Domiŧio Calderino: & Christoforo
Zaroto...repies.

296 × 207 mm.   With cuts.
Binding.   Vellum.
Provenance.   Signature of 'Giaco: Soranzo. 1724'; with bibliographical note
  inserted.
Essling 1141.

207.   VITRUVIUS.   De architectura.   Johannes Tacuinus.   22
May 1511.   Fᵒ.

Edited by Johannes Jucundus.   The first illustrated edition.
[*Title* in caps.]   M. Vitruvius per Iocundum solito castigatior factus cum
  figuris et tabula ut iam legi et intelligi possit (within border).   [Fol. 2]
  Dedication to Julius II.   [Col.] Impressum Venetiis...diligentia Ioannis
  de Tridino alias Tacuino.   Anno Domini. M.D.XI. Die. xxii. Maii *etc.*
310 × 213 mm.   Some marginal annotations (about 1600) in a hand not unlike
  that of Abraham Ortelius.
Binding.   Modern red morocco, gilt edges.
Provenance.   Bought of Ellis 16 May 1867.   R. C. Hussey (†1887)[1].
Brunet V. 1327.   Essling 1702.

208.   PETRARCA.   Li Sonetti Canzone Triumphi.   B. Stagnino.
May 1513.   4ᵒ.

With the commentaries of Philelphus and Ilicinus.
Two volumes (in 1).   The title and sixth leaf of Vol. II inserted from a
  smaller copy.   In Vol. I is a full-page woodcut of Cupid crowning
  Petrarch; and in Vol. II six cuts illustrating the Trionfi.
213 mm.
Binding.   Modern half-vellum.
Provenance.   Agostino Caironi, Milano (stamp).   J. and J. Leighton (1905
  catalogue), no. 3943.
Brunet IV. 545.   Essling 86.

209.   PETRARCA.   Opere.   Augustino de Zanni.   20 May
1515.   Fᵒ.

With the commentaries of Ilicino on the Trionfi; Philelphus, Antonio de
  Tempo, Hieronimo Alexandrino, on the Sonetti and Canzone 'nouamente
  historiate: e correcte per misser Nicolo Peranzone.'
288 × 200 mm.
Binding.   Plain vellum.
Provenance.   Laurencij Lataroli.
Essling 87.

[1] Not in Sale Catalogue.

210. LUCRETIUS. De rerum natura. In aedibus Aldi et Andreae Soceri. Mense Januario 1515. 8º.

The second Aldine edition.
154 mm.
Binding. Old mottled calf.
Provenance. Hamilton Palace (1884), no. 1237. Quaritch.
Brunet III. 1218. Renouard 74 (11).

211. HISTORIAE AUGUSTAE SCRIPTORES. In aedibus Aldi et Andreae Soceri. Mense Iulio 1516. 8º.

Edited by J. B. Egnatius.
161 mm.
Binding. Red morocco gilt (modern), with Aldine stamp on side as on no. 139.
Provenance. Longman. Syston Park (1884), with bookplates.
Brunet III. 225. Renouard 76 (4).

212. SAVONAROLA. Triumphus crucis. Lucas Olchiensis. 8 June 1517. 8º.

Fratris Hieronymi. | Savonarolæ, Ferrariensis, Ordinis prædicato-|rum, Triumphus crucis, de fidei ueritate. | *etc.* [Cut on title] [Col.] Venetiis... per Lucā olchīensem artium & legum professorem...M.CCCCCXVII. Die uero octavo mēsis Iunii.
140 mm. Ff. cxii.
Binding. Half-vellum, paper sides.
Provenance. J. and J. Leighton.
Brunet V. 161. Essling 1452. Cf. Audin 17–19.

213. OVIDIUS. Metamorphoses. Georgio Rusconi. 20 May 1517. Fº.

Italian translation.
The title in a compartment similar in style to that of no. 205, and the first leaf of text (fol. 5) surrounded with border pieces.
312 × 205 mm.
Binding. Olive morocco.
Provenance. William Howard (bookplate).
Cf. Brunet IV. 293 (not this edition). Essling 231.

214. BIBLIA LATINA. Lucas Antonius de Giunta. 15 October 1519. 8º.

Biblia cum concordantijs veteris & | noui testamenti *etc.* With woodcuts. 149 mm.

Binding. Contemporary stamped pigskin. 'Hic est filius' (Baptism in Jordan) etc. on front cover, 'Ecce virgo concipies' (Annunciation) on back. Clasps.

Provenance. Bookstamp of 'Agostino Caironi Milano' on title.

Renouard 60. Copinger, *Inc. Bibl.* (App. p. 212). Essling 145.

215. DANTE. La Divina Comedia. B. Stagnino. 25 March 1520. 4º

Opere del divino | poeta Danthe con suoi comenti: | recorrecti et con ogne di-|ligentia novamente in | littera cursiva | impresse. [Col.] Fine del comento di Christoforo Landino...reuista...per...Pietro da Figino... Impressa in Venetia per Miser Bernardino stagnino da Trino de monferra. Del. M.CCCC.XX. A di .XXVIII. Marzo.

Ff. (12) + 1-438, 440-441. With cuts. A reprint of the edition of 1512. 217 mm.

Binding. Brown calf, by J. Mackenzie 'Bookbinder to the King.'

Provenance. J. and J. Leighton (1905 catalogue), no. 1394.

Koch p. 7. Essling 539.

216. ——. Another copy.

The preliminary matter (twelve leaves) in this copy is from a copy of the edition of 1512. On the title the cut of St Bernardino is to left, and the side-pieces differ. 212 mm.

Binding. Half-calf.

Provenance. Autograph of 'Thomas H. Cromek. Rome 1837-8. To his friend Edwd. Cheny Dec. 5, 1866.' With printed monogram and motto of E. Cheny inserted. Lot 705 in some sale.

217. DANTE. La Divina Comedia. Jacopo del Burgofranco for L. A. Giunta. 23 January 1529. Fº.

With commentary of Landino. With cuts. ' The title within border-pieces. 309 × 205 mm.

Binding. Red calf with blind tooling (saec. XVII?), rebacked.

Provenance. 'Ex libris Amaltheorum (?)' on title.

Koch p. 7. Essling 542.

218. PURBACH (GEORG). Novæ Theoricæ Planetarum.
M. Sessa. 1534. 8º.

NOVÆ THEO|RICÆ PLANETARUM GEORGII PEUR-|bachii Astronomi cele-
berrimi : Temporis importunitate | & hominum iniuria locis compluribus
conspurca-|tæ, a PETRO. Apiano Mathematicæ rei Ordi-|nario Ingol-
stadiano iam ad omnē veritatē | redactæ, & eruditis figuris illustratæ.
[Figure.] [Col.] Impressum Venetiis per Melchiorem Sessa. Anno
Domini M.D.XXXIIII.
Dedicated by Apianus to Georg Tanstetter.
Ff. 40 ('39' bis). With numerous figures.
149 mm.
Binding. Paper cover.
Provenance. Not recorded.
Houzeau et Lancaster, I. 551.

219. COSMOGRAPHIAE INTRODUCTIO. J. A. de Nicolinis de
Sabio, sumpt. Melchioris Sessae. January 1535. 8º.

COSMO|GRAPHIÆ INTRODUCTIO | cum quibusdam Geometriæ ac Astro- |
nomiæ principiis ad eam | rem necessarijs. [Figure.] M.D.XXXV. [Col.]
Venetijs per Io. Antonium de Nicolinis de Sabio, | sumptu & requisitione
D. Melchioris | Sessæ. Anno Domini. | M.D.XXXV. | Mensis Ianuarij.
Ff. 31+(1). Several figures, and mark of Sessa on last leaf.
149 mm. For the author of this work, Waldsee-Müller, grecized as Hyla-
comylus, and for earlier editions see Brunet.
Binding. Old vellum, recased.
Provenance. Not recorded.
Cf. Brunet II. 316. Cf. Fr. R. v. Wieser, *Die Cosmographiae Introductio
des M. Waldseemüller in Faksimiledruck*, Strassburg, 1907.

220. MAURO FIORENTINO. Sphera Volgare. B. Zanetti,
1537. 4º.

From the Latin of Johannes de Sacro Bosco.
[A 1] Arms of Charles V in border. [A 1 b] Elegiac couplet. [A 2] Sphera
volgare novamente | tradotta con molte notande | additioni di geo-
metria, cosmo-|graphia, arte navigatoria, et | stereometria, proportioni
...Autore M. Mauro Fiorentino Phonasco et philopanareto. | A Messer
Giovan' Orthega | Di Carion Burgense Hispano, & Dino | Compagni
Patritio Fiorentino, | Mathematici. [In zodiacal compartment, with coat
of arms.] [A 2 b] Whole page illustration of the author. [A 3 a] Dedication to Giovan' Orthega di Carion. [Col. O 4 a] M.D.XXXVII. Mense
Ottobri, &c. | Impresso in Venetia per Bartholomeo Zanetti ad instantia
& requisitione | di M. Giouam' Orthega de Carion Burgense Hyspano |
Comorante in Firenze. [O 4 b] Arms of Ortega, followed by Correttioni
(one leaf), and figure of the Pole star and little Bear on separate leaf

above which there is a blind impression of the block of the mariner's compass used on sig. N 2 *b*.

58 leaves.   215 mm.

Binding.   Niger morocco, blind tooled, by J. and J. Leighton.

Provenance.   J. and J. Leighton (1905 catalogue), no. 267.

Cf. Essling 257–268.

221.   BIRINGUCCIO (VANOCCIO).   De la Pirotechnia.   V. Roffi-nello.   1540.   4°.

The first edition.   Reprinted in 1558; translated and printed in French in 1556, 1572 and 1627.   Another copy in the Library.

[1 *a*] De la piro-|technia. | Libri. x....Composti per il S. Vanoc-|cio Birin-guccio Sennese. | ...M.D.XL. [In a compartment.] [1 *b*] Al...Bernardino di Moncelesi da Salo, Curtio Navo. [Printer's mark at foot.] [Col.] Stampata in Venetia per Venturino Roffinello. Ad instantia di Curtio Navo. & Fratelli. Del. M.CCCCC.XL.

Ff. (8)+168.   Many figures in the text.

204 mm.

Binding.   Contemporary vellum.

Provenance.   On the title the autograph signature of 'Hellot,' qu. the translator of Schlutter's *De la Fonte des Mines*?

Brunet I. 954.

222.   DANTE.   La Divina Comedia.   F. Marcolini.   June 1544.   4°.

The first edition of Vellutello's commentary (see Koch).   This copy is one of those in the extremely rare state, without the three lines, Purgatorio II. 64—66, generally inserted by hand-printing.   87 woodcuts.   These are entirely different from all previous illustrations.   Another copy in the Library.

Title in caps.: La comedia di Dante | Aligieri con la no-|va esposiṭǐone di | Alessandro Vellutello. [Col.] Impressa in Vinegia per Francesco Marcolini ad instantia di Alessandro Vellutello del mese di Gugno lanno M.D.XLIIII.

223 mm.

Binding.   Old vellum.

Provenance.   Not recorded.

Koch I. 8.   Essling 545.

223.   BOIARDO (MATTEO MARIA).   Orlando Innamorato.   Heredi di Lucantonio Giunta.   1545.   4°.

On the peculiarities of this edition, see Brunet.   It is inferior to that of 1541. The first 82 stanzas are new, and excel the original 80 of the editions of 1541 and 1542.

ORLANDO | INNAMORATO COMPOSTO | GIA DAL. S. MATTEO MARIA
BOIARDO | CONTE DI SCANDIANO, | Et hora rifatto tutto di nuovo da
M. Francesco Berni. | ... | Aggiunte in questa seconda editione molte
stanze | del autore che nelaltra mancauano. | [Mark.] | ... | M.D.XLV.
[Col.]...Venetia per li heredi di Lucantonio Giunta, ne l' anno del
Signore. M.D.XLV. Nel mese di Giugnio.
213 mm.
Binding. Old vellum. Arms of Pope Pius VI (1775-1798) stamped in
gold on the sides.
Provenance. See above.

224. BOIARDO. Another copy.
216 mm.
Binding. Mottled calf with gilt dentelle corners and gilt back, HP and
earl's coronet on four panels; and S and earl's coronet pasted on the fifth.
Provenance. Signature of Lionardo Dati. Bookplates of Henrietta Countess
of Pomfret (d. 1761); Second Earl of Shelburne (1737-1805); Rev. Walter
Sneyd (1903), lot 113.
Brunet I. 1051. Renouard, p. xxxi. Cf. Essling 1545.

225. PETRARCA. [Opere.] G. Giolito. 1545. 4°.

According to Brunet, this is perhaps the best of the numerous editions of
this commentary. There are two issues of this edition, of which this is
the second. The other state has 1543 in the colophon.
Il Petrarcha | Con l' espositione | d' Alessandro Vellutello | di novo ristam-
pato con le figu-|re ai triomphi, et con piu cose] utili in varii luoghi
aggiunte.|In Vinegia appres|so Gabriel Giolito|de Ferrari|MDXXXXV. |
[Col.] MDXLV. (All in capitals.)
Title in very ornate compartment as in no. 226.
Ff. (8)+197+(7). Preface by Lodovico Domenichi.
211 mm.
Binding. Vellum (saec. XVIII).
Provenance. From Samuel Rogers's Library.
Brunet IV. 551. Essling 106.

226. PETRARCA. [Opere.] G. Giolito. 1547 (1548). 4°.

The sixth edition. Ff. (8)+216+(30). The last 30 leaves contain, with
fresh title, 'Espotione di tutte i vocaboli, et luoghi difficili...Raccolte da
M. Ludovico Dolce, e da lui stesso corrette et ampliate in questa sesta
editione:...MDXLVIII.' Title and cuts as in no. 225.
221 mm.
Binding. Very handsome crimson morocco with richest arabesque tooling
of the sixteenth century on the sides, but inlaid and rebacked. Qu.
Nicolas Eve?
Provenance. E. H. Lawrence (1892), lot 505.
Brunet IV. 551. Cf. Essling 107-8

227. PTOLEMAEUS. Geografia. N. Bascarini for G. B. Pedrezano. 1548 (1547). 8º.

Ptolemeo | La Geografia | di Claudio Ptolemeo | Alessandrino, | Con alcuni
comenti & aggiunte fat|teui da Sebastiano munstero Ala|manno, Con
le tauole non solamente | antiche & moderne solite di stāpar-|si, ma
altre nuoue aggiunteui di Me|ser Iacopo Gastaldo Piamōtese cos-|mo-
grapho, ridotta in uolgare Italia|no da M. Pietro Andrea Mat-|tiolo
Senese medico Eccellētissimo | ... In Venetia, per Gioā. Baptista
Pedrezano...M.D.XLVIII. [With border-pieces.] [F. 215] In Venetia, ad
Instantia di messer Giouā Battista Pedrezano | libraro al segno della
Torre a pie del ponte di Rialto. | Stampato per Nicolo Bascarini nel
Anno del | Signore. 1547. del mese di Ottobre. [Bookseller's mark.]
2 Pts. Ff. (8)+214+(2); 60 double leaves, containing 2-page plates en-
graved on metal, +(64 leaves of table).
166 mm.
Binding. Brown marbled parchment paper boards.
Provenance. At foot of title the autograph: 'Benedicti Benzoni. ll. Doct.
Carthusie Venetiarum.'
Brunet IV. 956. Justin Winsor, *Bibliography*, pp. 24—28. Essling 1700.

228. SCAINO (ANTONIO). Trattato del Giuoco della Palla.
G. Giolito et Fratelli. 1555. 8º.

TRATTATO | DEL GIVOCO DELLA | PALLA DI MESSER | ANTONIO SCAINO
DA | SALÒ, DIVISO IN | TRE PARTI... | [Mark.] | In Vinegia appresso
Gabriel | Giolito de' Ferrari, et | Fratelli. MDLV.
Pp. (32), 315+(5), with additional pages inserted 155*—158*, 157*—160*,
163*—174*, 177*—180 ('108')* containing woodcuts.
145 mm.
Binding. Brown calf, gilt back.
Provenance. British Museum duplicate (1831).
Haym III. 179 (8). Brunet V. 178.'

229. VENICE. Academia. Summa librorum. [P. Manutius.]
In Academia Veneta. 1559. 4º.

Summa librorum, | quos in omnibus scientiis, | ac nobilioribus artibus, |
variis linguis conscriptos, | vel antea nunquam divulgatos, | vel utilissimis,
et pulcherrimis scholiis, | correctionibus'que illustratos, | in lucem
emittet | Academia Veneta. | [Metal engraving.] In Academia Veneta, |
M.D.LIX.
Ff. (4)+39. An Italian edition of this was published in 1558, in folio.
Binding. French red morocco, gilt edges (saec. XIX).
Provenance. Qu. Guizot?
Renouard 270.

230. ARIOSTO. Orlando Furioso. V. Valgrisi. 1571. 4°.

Orlando Furioso di M. Lodovico Ariosto, tutto ricorretto, et di nuove figure adornato. Con le Annotationi...di Ieronimo Ruscelli. La Vita dell' Autore...dal Signor Giouan Battista Pigna...La dichiaratione di tutte le Istorie...fatta da M. Nicolò Eugenico. Di nuovo aggiuntovi Li Cinque Canti...In Venetia, Appresso Vincenzo Valgrisi. M.D.LXXI.

Pp. (16)+654+(34). The title in an elaborate compartment.

At p. 533 'I cinque Canti...con gli argomenti...et discorsi Di M. Luigi Grotta d' Adria' with new title, and at p. 589 'Stanze del signor Luigi Gonzaga, detto Rodomonte.'

239 mm.

Binding. Old Italian vellum, blue edges.

Provenance. On the title is the heraldic bookstamp of a previous owner (Italian?) of noble family, not yet identified. On the penultimate page a MS. note: '1649 25 Aprile Jo. Andrea. Questo libro è di me Gio: Negri' with his coat of arms.

Cf. Brunet I. 434. Cf. Essling 2243 sqq.

231. BELLINATO (FRANCESCO). Discorso di Cosmografia. Presso Aldo. 1595. 8°.

Title. Discorso di cosmografia, in dialogo. Doue si ha piena notitia...di tutto 'l Mondo. Nuouamente stampato....In Venetia. CIꝐ.IꝐ.XCV. Presso Aldo.

Pp. 48+(6). The last six pages contain a list of books from the Aldine press, on sale at Venice in 1594.

140 mm.

Binding. Red morocco (early XIX cent.), gilt tooled, gilt edges, silk lining.

Provenance. Syston Park (1884), no. 719, with bookplates.

Renouard 252.

SWITZERLAND

BASEL

232. MÜNSTER (SEBASTIAN). Organum Uranicum. Hen.
Petri. March 1536. Fº.

Title. Organum Uranicum. Sebastianus Munsterus...Canones [with cut].
Collation. †, a–i, A–C⁴ D⁶ (D 6, blank?, gone). Movable discs attached to
A 1 *b*, A 2 *b*, A 3 *b*, A 4 *a* and *b*, B 1 *b* (gone), B 2 *a*, B 3 *b*, B 4 *a*, D 2 *a*.
MS. Italian notes inserted on a separate leaf after A 1, 3, and 4, and
C 1.
302 × 200 mm.   Not coloured.
Binding. Paper boards.
Provenance. Catalogue no. 62,825.
Panzer VI. 313. 1073.   BM (coloured plates).

FRANCE

PARIS

233. HEURES a l'usaige de Rome. P. Pigouchet pour G. Eustace. 1509. 8°.

[a 1] [Mark of Eustace.] Ces presètes heures a lusaige de Rōme | au long sans requerir ont este imprimees a | Paris par Philippe pigouchet / pour Guil|laume eustace marchant Libraire: demou-|rant a Paris en la rue de la iuifrie a lensai|gne des sagittaires ou dedēs la grāde salle | du palais au tiers pillier. Mil. V.C. & .IX.

Collation. [a]–q⁸ r⁴ ✠⁴. On vellum. Quire signature 'r' (Rome). Large illustrations coloured and gilded. Borders not coloured.

182 mm.

Binding. Common red morocco, gilt (ab. 1840), with the owner's initials 'B.L.' under a viscount's coronet on sides. A modern metal clasp, with miniature of Our Lord with crown of thorns and reed; the catch gone.

Provenance. French. See binding.

Panzer VII. 536. 310. Brunet V. 1646. Bohatta 809.

234. PARALDUS (Gulielmus). Summa virtutum ac vitiorum. J. Barbier. 18 Dec. 1512. 8°.

Preliminary title. Summa virtutum ac vi|tiorum Guilhelmi peral|di Epis-cōpi Lugdunen. | de ordine p̄dicatorum. *Second title.* [a 1] Sūma vir-tu-|tum ac vitiorū Guilhelmi Paral-|di Episcopi Lugdunensis de ordi-|ne predicatorum. | [J. Frellon's mark.] | Venundantur Parisius a Johanne Frellon in vico | di-ui Maturinorum sub signo vulgariter nūcupato | La cage. [Col.]...per Joannē Barbier librarium Parisiēn. iuratum Impensis vero...Joannis petit. Joannis Frellon et Fancisci (*sic*) regnault. Anno... M.CCCCC. 12. 15 calēdas Januarij.

Four parts. I. Preliminary, 8 leaves (last two blank). II. Sūma virtutum &c. (as above). 275+(17) leaves (last gone). III. Summarium, 34 leaves. IV. Annotatio, 232 leaves.

157 mm.
Binding. Vellum (xvii cent.) with stamp 'P. F. Ioannes Bocquet S.T.M.'
and coat of arms.
Provenance. See binding. Signatures of 'Johannes Hildebrant' and many
other previous owners, apparently Dominicans at Antwerp.
Panzer X. 7. 520 b.

235. TURRECREMATA (JOANNES DE). Tractatus contra prin-
cipales errores Mahometi & Turchorum. G. Eustace. [Ab.
1510?] 8⁰.

Tractatus contra princi-|pales errores ꝑfidi machometi & turcho℣ | siue
sarraceno℣ festināter copulatus ꝑ re|uerēdissimū dominū Johannem de
turre cremata | romane eccl'ie tituli sancte marie trās tyberī pre-|sbyterū
cardinalē sancti sixti vulgariter nūcupatū | [Mark of Eustace.] | ❡ Venū-
daī Parisi⁹ ī vico Judaico sub signo duo|rū Sagittario℣ : aut in palacio
regio tertio pilari.
Ff. 56.   176 mm.
Binding. Brown calf (xviii cent.). With nos. 236 and 237.
Provenance. 'Crofts sale May 1783. 10. 6.' Guy Phillips (bookplate).
William Morris (1898), lot 1033.
Panzer VIII. 219. 2819.

236. SAMUEL (RABBI). Tractatus contra Judeos. G. Eustace.
[Ab. 1510?] 8⁰.

❡ Tractatus cōtra iudeos a | quodā iudeo noīe samuel edi-|tus sermōe
arabico: trāslat⁹ | aūt ī latinuz a fratre alfontio. | [Mark of G. Eustace.]|
❡ Venūdantur Parisius in vi|co Judaico sub signo duorum | Sagittario℣ :
aut in Palatio | regio tertio Pilari.
Ff. 17+(1). [Second mark of Eustace at end.]
Binding. With nos. 235 and 237.
Provenance. Ibid.
Panzer VIII. 219. 2820.

237. DIALOGUS christiani contra sarracenum. G. Eustace.
[1510?] 8⁰.

Dyalogus christiani | contra sarracenum. | [Mark of G. Eustace.] | ❡ Venū-
dantur Parisius in vi|co Judaico sub signo duorum | Sagittario℣ : aut in
Palatio | regio tertio Pilari.
Ff. 35+(1). Second mark of Eustace at end.
Binding. With nos. 235 and 236.
Provenance. Ibid.
Panzer VIII. 219. 2821.

238. HORAE ad usum Romanum. T. Kerver. 5 December 1519. 8º.

[T. Kerver's mark.] | ❧ Hore deipare virginis Marie secundū vsum Roma| num / plerisq; biblie figuris atq; chorea lethi circūmu-|nite / nouisq; effigiebus adornate / ut in septē psalmis | penitentialib⁹ / in vigiliis defunctorū / & in horis sctē | crucis / in horis quoq; scti spūs videre licebit. 1519. | [Col.]...Anno dni Mil. cccccxix. die .v. mensis Decembris.
A–Q⁸ R⁴. On vellum. Text initials inserted by hand. All the cuts plain. No quire signature (cf. no. 233).
180 mm.
Binding. Purple morocco, gilt (saec. XIX).
Provenance. Henry Latham (1872), with bookplate.
At the foot of sig. I 7 b is written, under a monogram:

> 'Sy Jachepve ma grande ēprise
> Brief tu te verras (tost *erased*) la marquise.'

in a hand of the sixteenth century.
Note by G. Dotti, bookseller of Florence.
Bohatta 937.

239. ROMAN DE LA ROSE. Galliot Du Pré. 1531. Fº.

Clement Marot's third Recension III.
Title. Cy est le Rommant de la Roze *etc.* [Last leaf.] Mark of Galliot Du Pré.
275 × 196 mm. Cuts and initial letters (not coloured).
Binding. Blue morocco elaborately inlaid with conventional roses; end leaves of red watered silk. By Gottermayer N. Könyvkötö.
Provenance. Not recorded.
Brunet III. 1175. F. W. Bourdillon, pp. 32, 60, 61 (first state). The Library, New Series, Vol. IX, p. 143 (article by A. Tilley).

240. LE FEVRE (RAOUL). Le Recueil des Histoires Troyennes. D. Janot. 1532. Small Fº.

❧ Le recueil des hy|stoires Troyennes |...reueu et corrige nouuellement a la | vraye verite. | ❧ On les vend a Paris par Denis Ja-|not libraire Demourāt en la rue neuf|ue nostre Dame a lenseigne de les|cu de France. | M.D.XXXII. | [In a rough compartment.]
A–X, Aa–Ff⁶ (last leaf, containing the mark of Denis Janot, gone). Numerous cuts. The Yemeniz catalogue corrects the description in Brunet. The verso of the title contains a large woodcut. The name of the author is on the second leaf.

240 mm.
Binding. Green morocco by H. Duru, gilt by Thompson.
Provenance. Yemeniz (1867) 2335. Seillière (1887), no. 627.
Panzer VIII. 160. 2177. Brunet III. 926.

241. VEGETIUS RENATUS (FLAVIUS). Du fait de guerre, &c.
C. Wechel. 1536. Fᵒ.

Title. Flaue Vegece Rene...du fait de guerre: et fleur de cheualerie. quatre
   livres. Sexte Jule Frontin...des Stratagemes / especes / & subtilitez de
   guerre / quatre liures. Aelian de lordre et instruction des batailles. vng
   liure. Modeste des vocables du fait de guerre. vng liure. Pareillement.
   cxx. histoires...Traduicts...de latin en francois: & collationez (par le
   polygraphe...historien du parc dhonneur [N. Wolkyr[1]]) aux liures
   anciens / tant a ceulx de Bude / que Beroalde / et Bade. [Printer's mark.]
   Jmprime a Paris par Chrestien wechel...M.D.XXXVI. Fᵒ.
318 × 212 mm. Woodcuts. Initial letters. Ff. (12) + 320 + (2).
Binding. Dark blue morocco by Capé. Gilt edges.
Provenance. Ellis, 1866.
Panzer VIII. 198. 2588. Brunet V. 1162.

242. HEURES à l'usage de Rome. Jacques Kerver. 1558. 8ᵒ.

℃ Heures de nostre Dame a lusage | de Romme / Nouuellement imprimees
   a Pa-|ris / auec plusieurs belles histoires / tant au Ka-|lendrier / aux heures
   nostre Dame / aux heures de la Croix / aux heures du sainct Esprit:
   aux | sept psalmes / que aux Vigiles. | [T. Kerver's mark.] |
¶ A Paris par Iacques Keruer demeurant en la grand Rue | sainct Iacques,
   à l'enseigne de la Licorne. [Col.] M.d.lviij.
ab℃c–z⁸. 'Fo. clxxxiij' + (1). Single column. Many cuts. Signature
   title 'Rom̄.'
164 mm.
Binding. Stamped leather, in the manner of the sixteenth century.
Provenance. Not recorded.
Cf. Brunet V. 1627.

243. SCRIPTORES HISTORIAE ROMANAE. H. Stephanus.
1568. 8ᵒ.

Varii Historiæ Romanae Scriptores, partim Græci, partim Latini, in vnum
   velut corpus redacti, De rebus gestis ab Vrbe condita, vsque ad imperii
   Constantinopolin translati tempora...Anno M.D.LXVIII excudebat Henricus
   Stephanus.

----

[1] For Nicholas Wolkyr or Volcyre de Serouville see Brunet.

4 voll.   Misbound.   The 8 preliminary leaves of vol. I are followed by the
contents of vol. 2.   The contents of vol. I are bound as vol. 4.   Vols. 3
and 4 are lettered 2 and 3.
165 mm.
Binding.   Olive morocco, gilt, with the arms (not identified) of the owner
with his monogram 'LB,' qu. Bailly? (cf. Guigard) (XVII cent.).
Provenance.   See binding.
Renouard, 131–2.   Cf. Brunet V. 243–4.

244.   ARISTOTELES.   Opera omnia (Graecé et Latine).   Lute-
tiae Parisiorum Typis Regiis.   1619.   Large Fº.

Title.   ARISTOTELIS OPERA OMNIA QUÆ EXTANT Graecè & Latinè.   Ve-
terum ac recentiorum interpretum, ut Adriani Turnebi, Isaaci Casauboni,
Iulij Pacij, studio emendatissima.   CVM KYRIACI STROZÆ PATRITII
FLORENTINI LIBRIS DUOBUS Græcolatinis de Republicâ in supplementum
Politicorum Aristotelis...accessit...Commentarius...Authore GVILLIELMO
DV VAL...qui...adjecit Anthologiam Anatomicam ex scitis Hippocratis &
Galeni...& praeterea libros quatuordecim diuinioris Philosophiæ seu
Metaphysicorum, notis & argumentis auxit ac...restituit *etc.*
In two volumes.
411 mm.
Binding.   Red morocco with plain gold tooling, by Duseuil.
Provenance.   'Ex libris Augustini de Maupeou' (bookplate).
Brunet I. 459.

LYONS

245.   VERGILIUS.   [Æneid and minor works.]   J. Crespin for
Vincent de Portonariis.   1529.   Fº.

Title.   Aeneis Virgiliana.   Cum Servii...commentariis, cum Philippi Beroaldi
...annotationibus...Cum Donati...enodationibus, Cum Augustini Dathi...
introductione.   Cū'qꝫ...Iodoci Badii Ascensii elucidatione...Accessit...
Mapphei Veggii liber...Adiectas nuperrime comperies castigationes...
per...Ioannem Pierium Valerianum ... Permulta ... in enarrationibus
Christophori Lādini...reperies.   [Bookseller's mark : Vincentius de Portonariis de Tridino de Monte Ferrato.]...M.D.XXIX.   [Col.]   Lugduni in...
officina Joannis Crespini...M.D.XXIX.   Fº.
Another edition of that printed at Lyons in 1517 (BM)
306 × 205 mm.   Cuts and initial letters.
Binding.   Maroon morocco, with gilt edges, by R. Petit.
Provenance.   Renatus Benedictus Prioul, humanista, 1685.
Panzer VII. 346. 595.   Cf. Baudrier V. 437.   Renouard, *Jose Bade,* III. 377.

246. DONI (ANTONIO FRANCESCO).   Les mondes, celestes, terrestres et infernaux.   E. Michel.   1580.   8º.

> Les Mondes, Celestes, Terrestres et Infernaux. Le Monde petit, Grand, Imaginé, Meslé, Risible, des Sages & Fols, & le Tresgrand, L'Enfer des Escoliers, des mal Mariez, des Putains & Ruffians, des Soldats & Capitaines poltrons, des pietres Docteurs, des Vsuriers, des Poëtes & Compositeurs ignorans: Tirez des œuures de Doni Florentin, par Gabriel Chappuis Tourangeau. Depuis, reueuz, corrigez & augmentez du Monde des Cornuz, par F[rancois]. C[hapuis]. T[ourangeau]. [Printer's mark.]   A. Lyon, pour Estienne Michel, 1580.   8º.

2 Parts. Pp. (16)+476 (477)+(9); 264. The second edition. Complimentary verses prefixed.

168 mm.

Binding.   Crushed red morocco by Chambolle-Duru.   Gilt edges.

Provenance.   Not recorded.

Brunet II. 811–2.

HOLLAND

LEIDEN

247. MANILIUS (M.). Astronomicon. C. Rapheleng. 1599 (1600). 4°.

> M. Manill Astronomicon a Iosepho Scaligero ex vetusto codice Gembla-censi...repurgatum. Eiusdem Iosephi Scaligeri Notæ...Ex officina Plantiniana, Apud Christophorum Raphelengium, Academiae Lugduno-Batauae Typographum. CIↃ.IↃ.IC. [Col.] Lugd. Batavorum...Expensis Ioannis Commelini. Anno CIↃ.IↃ.C.
>
> Pp. (32)+510+(2).
> *Binding.* Old calf.
> *Provenance.* Not recorded.
> Dibdin, *Introduction* (1827) II. 224. Houzeau et Lancaster, I. 447.

248. HONDIUS (JUDOCUS). Nova et accurata Italiæ Hodiernæ Descriptio. B. et A. Elzeviri, 1627. Oblong F°.

> Nova et accurata Italiæ Hodiernæ Descriptio In qua omnium eius regionum ...historia exhibetur. Geographicis tabulis et urbium precipuarum iconibus illustrata a Iudoco Hondio Addita est Siciliæ, Sardiniæ, Corsicæ, et itinerariorum per Italiam brevis delineatio. Lugduni Batavorum Apud Bonavonturam (sic) et Abrahamum Elsevir Academiæ tijpograph. 1627. (Engraved title.)
>
> Pp. (8)+406+(2). Dedicated to the Doge and Senate of Venice. The plates are in the text. Extra plates are inserted to face pp. 304, 328, 340, 360.
> 213×276 mm.
> *Binding.* Old red morocco, gilt.
> *Provenance.* Sale no. 343.
> Willems, 74 (no. 279).

BELGIUM

ANTWERP

249. ORTELIUS (ABRAHAM).   Theatrum Orbis Terrarum.
[Col.] Antverpiæ, in officina Plantiniana, Auctoris ære et cura.
1592. Fº.

Titles. [Part 1.] THEATRUM ORBIS TERRARUM. Opus nunc denuo ab ipso
Auctore recognitum, multisquè locis castigatum, & quamplurimis nouis
Tabulis atquè Commentarijs auctum. [Part 2.] PARERGON, SIVE VE-
TERIS GEOGRAPHIÆ ALIQVOT TABULÆ. [Part 3.] NOMENCLATOR
PTOLEMAICVS; OMNIA LOCORVM VOCABVLA, QVÆ IN TOTA PTOLEMAEI
Geographia occurrunt, continens: ad fidem Græci codicis purgatus, & in
ordinem non minùs vtilem quàm elegantem digestus. ANTVERPIÆ, IN
OFFICINA PLANTINIANA, Sumptibus Abrahami Ortelij, Cosmographi
Regij. M.D.XCI. [Col.] ANTVERPIÆ, IN OFFICINA PLANTINIANA, AUC-
TORIS ære & cura. M.D.XCII.

Collation. [Part 1.] AB⁶, folding maps 1–108. [Part 2.] a⁴, folding maps
1–26. [Part 3.] A–F⁶ G⁸ (last leaf gone, blank?).

First published in 1570.

448 mm.   The maps and initial letters finely coloured by hand.

Binding. Red morocco binding (saec. XIX), richly gilt, with the Tennant
bookstamp.

Provenance. W. Tennant.

Brussels, *Bibl. Hulthem.* 14327.   Cf. Brunet IV. 242.

AUSTRIA

VIENNA

250. MISSALE PATAVIENSE. Ioannes Winterburger. 29 January 1509. 4°.

The ninth Passau missal.

[Fol. 1a] Missale Patauieñ. [Col.] Missale sm chorū Patauieñ...Joānes Winterburger ciuis Vienneñ. impͤssit & feliciter finiuit: anno christi. M.d.ix. Mensis Januarij die xxix. In Vienna Pannonia. [4 verses and printer's mark.]

Ff. (10)+272. Full-page woodcuts on verso of title and before Canon. Small cuts on sig. k 8 and historiated woodcut initials.

189 mm.

Binding. Contemporary pig-skin binding.

Provenance. 'Ad Franciscanos Eggenfeld Bibl. superior' (fol. 2), & 'Sum M. Melchioris Staudneri P. Eggenfeldae' (fol. 1). F. H. Dickinson (1886) lot 227.

Weale, 121. M. Denis I. 23 (no. 25).

SPAIN

TOLEDO

251. SENECA. Epistolas. P. Hagenbach. 5 March 1502. Fº.

The second edition.

Title. Las Epistolas de Seneca cō una summa si quier introducion de philosophia moral en romance (por L. Arietino) con tabla.

Collation. a⁸ (wants a 3–6), b–l⁶ m⁸.

Col. [Fol. lxxiii *b*.] Emprimidas enla...cibdad de Toledo. Por maestro Pedro hagembach aleman. Año de Mil. & quinientos & dos años. a cinco dias de mes de Marzo.

The translation of Aretino's work is attributed to Fernan Perez de Guzman, by C. A. de La Serna Santander (Brunet).

Illustrations. On the title a woodcut of a scribe writing, within border-pieces. Printed initial letters.

269·5 mm.

Binding. Half-calf, with mottled paper sides.

Provenance. William Powell (bookplate).

C. Perez Pastor, *La Imprenta en Toledos*, Madrid, 1887, p. 24 (no. 27). Haebler *Early Printers*, 138. Brunet V. 284.

252. SENECA. Epistolas. 27 Sept. 1510. Fº.

Third edition.

Title. [Cut] Las epistolas de Senecà | etc. [Col. Fol. lxxiii b]...Empressas en la muy noble | cibdad de Toledo. Año de Mil. & quini-|entos & diez años. a veynte & siete dias d'l | mes de setiembre.

283 × 199 mm.

Binding. Half roan with cloth sides.

Provenance. Biblioteca de Salvá V.P.S. (bookstamp). William Morris, (1898), lot 1115. Sir Edward Sullivan (1900) bookplate.

C. Perez Pastor, *La Imprenta en Toledos*, p. 31 (no. 46). Salva *Catalogo* (1872), II. 815 (no. 4004).

VALENCIA

253. BRADWARDINUS (THOMAS). Arithmetica, &c. J. Joffré.
1503. F°.

Title. Preclarissimum mathematicarū opus | in quo continêtur...arismetica
& eiusdez geometria necnō|...Pisanicarturiensis perspectiua | q̄ cois
īscribiť cū...ioānis d' assia sup|eadē...cum figuris...emēdatū p...thomā
durā *etc.* [Col.]...questionib⁹ Enrici de Assia...Impressū Valē|tie per
Joannem iofre & expensis Hieronymi Amigueti xvmj Octobris | Anni
M.d.tercij. *Followed by* Michaelis ioannis benedicti equitis jurati in
laudem *etc.*

293 × 202 mm. Initial letters. Woodcuts in margin.

Binding. Paper wrapper.

Provenance. No. 305 in some catalogue.

J. Pastor Fuster, *Biblioteca Valenciana*, I. 46. D. E. Smith, *Rara Arithmetica*, p. 61.

ENGLAND

LONDON

254. PRIMER. T. Petyt [153–?]. 16⁰.

17 lines to the page. Page of type: 80+52 mm.
Fragment, consisting of the greater part of 16 leaves. Two small cuts.
No signatures preserved.
Used as the end-leaves of no. 253, printed (and bound?) by Petit.
Probably the same book as that indicated by Hoskins, of which a fragment
only, consisting of 32 leaves, is in the British Museum.
Binding. With no. 255.
Provenance. See no. 255.
Cf. Hoskins 154.

255. STATUTES. The great abredgement. T. Petit. 1542. 8⁰.

[Title] ⓒ The great | Abredgement of all the | Statutes of Englande | with
the abredgemētes of the | statutes made in the .xxxiij. yere | of...Hēry
the eyght *etc.* [In a compartment of four pieces.] [Col.] Imprynted
at † Londón in Paules church yarde | at the Sygne of the May-|dens
heed by Thomas Petyt. In the yere | of our Lorde | God. | M.D.XLij.
2 Pts. Ff. (8)+cccxxi+(9); xxx+(2). Some leaves still unopened.
With signature and mottoes of Walter Mildmay (founder of Emmanuel
College) 'La vita fugge & non s'arresta vn' hora' and 'Virtute non
vi' on the title. The end-papers consist of part of an English primer
(no. 254).
Binding. Original stamped leather.
Provenance. Walter Mildmay (xvi cent.). Earl of Westmorland (1887),
no. 795 with label.

256. HARDYNG (JOHN). The Chronicle. R. Grafton. 1543. 8⁰.

[The Chronicle of John Hardyng, from the first beginning of Englande, unto
the reigne of Kyng Edward the fourth...And from that tyme is added a
continuation...in prose...now first imprinted...Londini Ex officina
Richardi Graftoni Mense Januarij M.D.xliii.]

Collation. ??⁸, a–z, A–F⁸ G⁶, Aa–Ss⁸ Tt².

The title, Ff. cxiii–cxx, cliiii–clix, clxi–clxxvii, clxxxv–cxcii, of the first part, and cxliiii–cxlvi (end) of the second part are reprinted (ab. 1820?).

A few MS. annotations in early hands.

191 mm.

Binding. Russia leather, gilt (about 1820).

Provenance. Richard West (ab. 1600), qu. the poet? See D.N.B. G. Hall.

Herbert 518–9. BM. 770 (two editions).

257. GOWER (JOHN). De confessione amantis. Thomas Berthelet, 12 March 1554. F°.

The third edition. The title in Berthelet's compartment with the Greek 'key' pattern border.

267 mm. This copy wants the blank leaf at end.

Binding. Black grained morocco with gilt tooling and gilt edges by C. Hering.

Provenance. John Fuller Russell (1885), with bookplate.

Herb. 456. BM. 714. ULC. 504.

258. SPENSER (EDMUND). The Faerie Queene. Books I–III. W. Ponsonbie. 1590. 4°.

The Faerie Queene. Disposed into twelue books, Fashioning XII. Morall vertues. London, Printed for William Ponsonbie, 1590. 4°.

The spaces on p. 332 left for the insertion of Welsh words are blank.

A–Z, Aa–Pp⁸ (paged 1–606). There is no Qq⁴.

Binding. Olive morocco, by W. Pratt (as 259).

Provenance. Not recorded.

Herb. 1273–4. BM. 1438. ULC. 1960.

259. SPENSER (EDMUND). The Faerie Queene. Books IV–VI. W. Ponsonby. 1596. 4°.

The Second Part of the Faerie Queene. Containing the Fourth, Fifth and Sixth Bookes. By Ed. Spenser. Imprinted at London for William Ponsonby, 1596.

179 mm.

Binding. Olive morocco, by W. Pratt (as 258).

Provenance. Not recorded.

Herb. 1275. BM. 1438. ULC. 2243.

260. GILBERT (WILLIAM). De magnete. P. Short. 1600. F°.

The first edition. With prefatory letter by Edward Wright.

With Denham's initial letters.

258 mm.

Binding. Plain brown calf (about 1800).

Provenance. 'P. Tho: Bourk So*cieta*tis Jesu Limer*icensis.*' J. Martin
    Leake (1863).
Herb. 1210. BM. 694. ULC. 2338.

261. SPEED (JOHN). The Theatre of the Empire of Great
Britaine. 1611, and are to be solde by John Sudbury and Georg
Humble. F^o.

The maps engraved by Jodocus Hondius in 1610 and 1611.
The name of Christopher Saxton is given on the maps of England, Norfolk,
    Worcestershire, Radnor, Montgomeryshire; that of John Norden on the
    maps of Kent, Surrey, Middlesex, Essex; that of William White on that
    of the Isle of Wight. The account of Norfolk was written by Sir Henry
    Spelman. The account of Scotland and Ireland dated 1611.
C. Savery's portrait of Speed engraved in 1629 is inserted loose in the volume.
    475 mm.
Binding. Whole russia binding, with gilt tooling, and bookstamp (the sun's
    rays issuant from clouds, beneath a chief, arms of LEESON) about 1840.
Provenance. See binding.
BM. 1435. Cf. ULC. 3215 (Scotland and Ireland 1612).

APPENDIX

FIFTEENTH CENTURY BOOKS FROM SOURCES OTHER THAN THE McCLEAN BEQUEST

GERMANY

MAINZ

PETER SCHOEFFER

262. BONIFACIUS VIII. Liber sextus decretalium, cum glossa. 9 Jan. 1476.· Large F°.

With the 'apparatus Joannis Andreae.'
Description in B.M.Catalogue.
Collation. Ibid.
407 × 287 mm. Capitals in blue and red. Initial strokes in red. Fine initial B on fol. 1 with figure of Boniface VIII on a burnished gold ground. Pinholes. Signatures in MS. Quire linings. MS. table of contents on a flyleaf.
Binding. Wooden boards covered with pigskin, with label on the front board (XV cent.). Five bosses all gone. Modern clasps. Mark of original chaining on the lower board.
Provenance. Name of early owner at top of fol. 1. A mutilated bookplate of a Dominican house. Munich Library duplicate. F. G. H. Culemann, 'Hanover 1842' (sale 1870). Bought at sale of W. H. Crawford of Lakelands (1891). Lot 417.
HC* 3593. Proctor 109. BM.Catalogue I. 32.

ERHARD REUWICH

263. BREYDENBACH (BERNHARD VON). Itinerarium. 11 February 1486. F°.

First Latin edition.
Description in Hain, BM.Catalogue, and Mr Hugh W. Davies' monograph.
Collation in BM.Catalogue.
310 mm. Capitals, paragraph marks and initial strokes in red. MS. signatures to quires. Margins much mended. Parts of the folding woodcuts of Venice and Jerusalem are in facsimile.
Binding. Old vellum.
Provenance. Purchased from a German bookseller in 1891.
H* 3956. Proctor 156. BM.Catalogue I. 43. H. W. Davies, *Bernhard von Breydenbach* (1911), p. 1. Schreiber, 3628.

STRASSBURG
JOHANN MENTELIN

264. THOMAS AQUINAS. Summa secunda secundae partis. [Not after 1466.] Fᵒ.

Description in Hain, BM.Catalogue.
Collation in BM.Catalogue. Sig. x 10 and y 7, 8 cut away (blanks).
400 mm. Capitals and paragraph marks in red or blue. In an initial P on the first leaf a very delicate miniature of St Thomas Aquinas writing his book.
Binding. Original wooden boards, with leather cover and blind tooling. Five brass bosses on each side, clasps (gone) and corner-pieces. Quire linings.
Provenance. On the inner side of the upper cover is the name and mark of 'P. Rinck' (15th cent.).
Purchased 1890.
H* 1454. Proctor 199. BM.Catalogue I. 51–52.

265. ALBERTUS MAGNUS. Opus virginis gloriosae. [About 1477–8.] Large Fᵒ.

Description in Hain, BM.Catalogue.
Collation in BM.Catalogue.
406 × 208 mm. An elaborate capital and footpiece on the third leaf. Ordinary capitals and initial strokes in red.
Binding. Maroon calf by Hering.
Provenance. Alexander I. Beresford Hope (1882) no. 169, with bookplate.
Presented by George Dunn, Esq., May 1909.
HC* 461. Proctor 229. BM.Catalogue I. 59.

JOHANN REINHARD OF GRÜNINGEN

266. TERENTIUS. Comediae. 11 February 1499. Fᵒ.

Description in Hain, and BM.Catalogue.
Collation in BM.Catalogue.
Illustrations. See Schreiber.
301 mm. Wants fol. i–xxiii, very many of the following leaves, and fol. clxx–clxxxi. Some leaves mutilated.
Binding. Modern half-calf.
Provenance. Evidently used in an English school in the 16th century. Scribbled names of Thomas Haryson (fol. lxiii and xciii), Thomas Ward and Thomas Strode (fol. xciii), William Beard (fol. clvi) and others, all of that period. Three signatures of T. Kerrich, Peterborough, 1825.
Bequeathed by the Rev. R. E. Kerrich, 1872.
H* 15432. Proctor 488. BM.Catalogue I. 113. Schreiber 5332.

267. TERENTIUS zü tütsch transferiert. 5 March 1499. Small F°.

First German translation.

Title. Terentius der Hochgelert vñ aller brüchlichest Poet. von latin zů tütsch Transferiert. nach dem text vnd nach der gloss. In sinē vi. büchern. Vs dē ein yeglicher mensch erkenē mag die sittē vnd gemüt d' andrē menschen. [Cut: Das huss der Comedien.]

Description. 300 × 205 mm. Rubricated. For woodcuts see Schreiber.

Collation. Copinger.

Binding. Original half-pig, wooden boards, with metal clasps.

Provenance. F. W. Heyse (?), Berlin 1841 (with signature). No. 3657. Bequeathed by C. Brinsley Marlay, 1912.

HC 15434. Proctor 489. BM.Catalogue I. 113. Schreiber 5333.

JOHANN PRÜSS

268. BOCCACCIO. Von den erlychten Frouen. 1488. F°.

The third edition of the German translation by Heinrich Steinhoewel of 'De praeclaris mulieribus.'

Description in Hain.

Collation. a⁸ (wants à 1), AB⁶ C⁸ D–N⁶ OP⁸ (last leaf blank).

Illustrations. With the cuts of the Ulm edition of 1473, except four and one new one. See Schreiber.

277 × 195 mm.

MS. inscription below the colophon: 'Messalina Claudij des Kaisers weib ging ins Gemein Hurhaus...Unkeuschem Willen zu erfullen.'

Binding. Original half-leather with blind tooling on plain wooden sides. Brass clasps. (With no. 282.)

Provenance. Signature of 'Hans Koburger (?) im Nurnberg (?) 1525' at head of the second leaf.

Purchased, Feb. 1890, from J. and J. Leighton.

H* 3336. Panzer *Annalen* I. 176 (269). R. Muther, *Deutsche Bücherillus-tration,* 514. Schreiber, 3509.

PRINTER OF THE 1483 IORDANUS DE QUEDLINBURG

269. DURANDUS. Rationale divinorum officiorum. [Not after 1483.] F°.

Description in Hain, BM.Catalogue.

Collation in BM.Catalogue. Ff. cxlvi, cxlvii, clvii, and clx supplied in contemporary handwriting.

293 mm.   Capitals and initial strokes in red.
Binding. Modern German paper.
Provenance. Bought from W. Ridler, 1892.
H* 6469.   Proctor 633.   BM.Catalogue I. 130.

MARTIN FLACH

270. NICOLAUS DE BLONE.   Tractatus sacerdotalis de sacra-
mentis. 1 October 1488. 4°.

Description in Hain, BM.Catalogue.
Collation in BM.Catalogue.
205 mm.   Capitals, paragraph marks and initial strokes in plain red.
Binding. Original leather with elaborate blind tooling, two lions back to
   back, pierced heart, swan, and Jhesus, Maria etc. Original clasps. Bound
   with nos. 335–337 (No. 3 in the volume).
Provenance. W. H. Crawford of Lakelands (1891) with bookplate. Bought
   at his sale, lot 2976.
H* 3253.   Proctor 676.   BM.Catalogue I. 148.

PRINTER OF THE CASUS BREVES
DECRETALIUM 1493
(G. HUSNER?)

271. MELBER (JOHANNES).   Vocabularius predicantium.
[About 1493–4.] 4°.

Description in Hain, BM.Catalogue.
Collation in BM.Catalogue.
208 mm.   Capitals in red, with flourishes.
Binding. Original wooden boards, covered with pigskin stamped with
   hound, boar, stag and rosette ; metal clasp.
Vellum flyleaves from a Breviary (XII cent.).
Provenance. Monasterii S... erarii. Cornelius Paine (1891) with signature
   bookplate. Bought 1891.
H* 11032.   Proctor 742.   BM.Catalogue I. 161.

COLOGNE
PRINTER OF AUGUSTINUS DE FIDE
(GOISWIN GOPS ?)

272. GERSON (JOHANNES).   De laude scriptorum.   [About 1473?]   4º.

Written about 1432 or 1433 at Lyons.
Description in Hain, BM.Catalogue.
Collation. [a⁸ b⁴.] Wants last four leaves.
200 × 141 mm. Plain red capitals.
Binding. Modern paper.
Provenance. Georg Kloss (1835), lot 1720, with bookplate.
Presented by George Dunn, Esq., May 1909.
HC. *7688. Proctor 1097. BM.Catalogue I. 233.

AUGSBURG
GÜNTHER ZAINER

273. RODERICUS ZAMORENSIS.   Speculum vitae humanae. 1471. Fº.

For two other copies and description and collation see nos. 70 and 70 A.
307 × 220 mm. Plain red capitals and initial strokes. The first capital in blue and red in the same manner as in the other two copies.
Wants one leaf (fol. 69).
Binding.
Provenance. (Inscription on first leaf:) 'Iste liber est monasterij S. Egidij Nurmberge. ordinis S. Benedicti. Emtus per venerabilem patrem dominum Sebaldum Helmasperger abbatem eiusdem monasterij. Anno domini.' Pinelli sale (April 1789).
M. Wodhull (1886), lot 2241. Bought from Leighton, 1891.
HC. *13940. Proctor 1525. BM.Catalogue II. 316.

274. RODERICUS ZAMORENSIS.   Spiegel des menschlichen lebens. [Not after 1473.] Fº.

Translated by Heinrich Steinhöwel. First illustrated edition.
Description in Hain, Morgan Catalogue.
Collation in Morgan Catalogue, and BM.Catalogue.
296 × 207 mm. Not rubricated.
Illustration. For the seventy-four woodcuts see W. Morris (in the Morgan Catalogue); S. C. Cockerell's *Woodcuts*, pp. 9, 10; and Schreiber 5102.

S. C.   8

Binding. Stamped pigskin of the 16th century, with leather thong ties. (Cf. the Morgan copy.)

Provenance. Edward Hailstone, F.S.A. (1891). Bought at his sale.

H. *13948. Proctor 1584. Morgan 139. BM. Catalogue II. 326. Schreiber 5102.

ANTON SORG

275. NIDER (JOHANN). Divine legis preceptorium. [About 24 May 1475.] F°

With the 'expositio decalogi.'

Description in Hain, BM.Catalogue.

Collation in BM.Catalogue.

286 mm. Capitals, paragraph marks and underlining in red.

Binding. Original wooden boards, covered with stamped leather (Augsburg). Metal bosses and clasps (one new). Lined with leaves of a paper Breviary (XV cent.).

Provenance. The Cistercian abbey of Georgenthal (Monasterij Montis S. Georgii), 1661.

Purchased Feb. 1891 (lot 93 in a sale).

H. *11789. Proctor 1642. BM.Catalogue II. 342.

276. BUCHLEIN von dem Leben unsers Herrn. 11 July 1491. F°.

Description in Hain.

Collation. a–r⁸. Wants sig. d 8 and e 1 (two leaves).

Illustration. Seventy woodcuts illustrating the Life of Christ. See Schreiber. 267 mm.

Inscription on title.

Binding. Modern half-calf, paper sides, by Mossly of Antwerp.

Provenance. Bought from Tregaskis, 1890.

H. *4060. Panzer *Annalen d. deutsch. Litt.* 309. Schreiber 3726.

JOHANN FROSCHAUER

277. SAVONAROLA. Expositio in psalmum Miserere. 1499. 4°.

Description. Expositio ac meditatio in psalmū | Miserere. fratris Hieronymi de Ferraria ordinis predi-|catorum. quam in vltimis diebus vite sue edidit.

Illustration. Crucifixion cut (120 × 90 mm.) on first leaf, recto and verso.

Collation. ab⁶.

199 × 135 mm.

Binding. Modern red velvet. Bound with thirteen other tracts of Savonarola[1].

Provenance. No. 4451 in some catalogue. Marlay bequest, 1912.

H. *14424. Proctor 1835. Audin 140. Schreiber 5199. Cf. BM. Catalogue II. 399.

NUREMBERG

ANTON KOBERGER

278. SCHEDEL (HARTMAN). Liber cronicarum. 1493. F°.

Another copy of no. 94, where see description, collation and notes.

420 × 292 mm. Wants ff. xii, xiii, and cclviiij–cclxi.

Binding. Modern half-leather.

Provenance. Viscount Fitzwilliam 1806, with signature.

Bequeathed by him in 1816.

279. ——. Another copy.

449 × 310 mm.

Binding. Mottled calf of the 18th century.

Provenance. Bookplate of Thomas Gaisford, Dean of Christ Church, Oxford (d. 1855).

Bequeathed by C. Brinsley Marlay, 1912.

280. BRIGITTA (S.). Revelationes. 21 September 1500. F°.

Edited by Florian Waldauf.

Description in BM.Catalogue.

Collation in BM.Catalogue. Wants sig. H 6 (blank).

An inscription (covered) on fol. 257 *b*.

Illustrations. Cf. R. Muther *Bücherillustration,* nos. 426–9; S. C. Cockerell, *Some German Woodcuts,* no. 84; and Schreiber.

Binding. 18th century marbled calf, with gold tooling (Italian).

Provenance. Giacomo Soranzo, 1742. Pinelli sale (April 1789). M. Wodhull (1886), lot 406, bought by Quaritch.

Bequeathed by C. Brinsley Marlay, 1912.

HC. 3205. Proctor 2124. BM.Catalogue II. 445. Schreiber 3504.

[1]

1.	Audin	57.	No. 312.	8. Audin	52 ?	No. 306.
2.	,,	29.	,, 310.	9. ,,	51.	,, 308.
3.	,,	93.	,, 313.	10. ,,	41.	,, 305.
4.	,,	97.	,, 311.	11. ,,	165.	,, 281.
5.	,,	28.	,, 309.	12. ,,	111.	,, 304.
6.	,,	38.	,, 314.	13. ,,	140.	,, 277.
7.	,,	54.	,, 307.	14. H. 14472		Not xv cent.

AMBROSIUS HUBER

281. POGGIUS (J. F.). Contra Fratrem Hieronymum. [After 1500 ?] 4⁰.

> *Description.* Contra Fratrem Hieronymum | Heresiarchā libellus et cessus.|
> [Cut: Savonarola seated writing, with three small devils at his ear.] |
> Nosce teipm̄. | [*Six verses.*]
> *Collation.* a⁸ b⁴ cd⁸.
> *Binding.* With no. 277. (No. 11 in the volume.)
> *Provenance.* 'Dnj Laurencij in Treuchtling est.' (Treuchtlingen near Eichstatt.)
> Bequeathed by C. Brinsley Marlay, 1912.
> H. *13386=14479. Copinger 4797. Proctor 3286. Audin 165. Schreiber 5001.

ULM

CONRAD DINCKMUT

282. LIRAR (THOMAN). Schwäbische Chronik. 12 January 1486. F⁰.

> *Description* in BM.Catalogue.
> *Collation* in BM.Catalogue. Wants sig. k 10.
> *Illustrations.* Twenty-one whole page illustrations, set out in Muther.
> 277 × 195 mm. Not rubricated.
> A MS. inscription below the colophon in the same hand and nearly in the same words as that in no. 268.
> *Binding* and *Provenance.* See no. 268.
> Purchased Feb. 1891.
> HC. *10117. Proctor 2567. Panzer *Deutsche Annalen*, 228. BM.Catalogue II. 535.
> Muther *Deutsche Bücherillustration*, 355. C. Fairfax Murray, *Early German Books*, 241. Schreiber 4508.

JOHANN REGER

283. CAOURSIN (GULIELMUS). Obsidio Rhodiae. 24 October 1496. F⁰.

> *Description* in Hain, BM., and Morgan Catalogues.
> *Collation.* a–f⁸ gh⁶.
> 277 × 195 mm. Marginal notes (XVI cent.).
> *Illustrations.* See R. Muther *Bücherillustration*, 367 ; and Schreiber 3667.

Binding. Old brown calf.
Provenance. W. H. Crawford of Lakelands (1891). Bought at his sale,
    lot 593.
HC. *4369. Proctor 2586. BM.Catalogue II. 542. Morgan Catalogue.
    Schreiber 3667.

REUTLINGEN

MICHAEL GREYFF

284. SPIEGEL menschlicher Behaltnis. [1 January?] 1492. F°.
With 'Evangelien und Epistelen.
Description in BM.Catalogue.
Collation in BM.Catalogue.
276 × 202 mm.
Illustrations. 270 woodcuts, some coloured. Woodcut initials. Woodcut
    frontispiece mounted.
Binding. Modern pigskin, imitation antique.
Provenance. W. H. Crawford of Lakelands (1891). Bought at his sale,
    lot 2987.
HC. 14938. Proctor 2739. BM.Catalogue II. 581. Schreiber 5280.

ITALY

ROME

GEORG LAUER

285. BERTACHINUS (JOHANNES). Repertorium utriusque juris. 1481. Large F⁰.

> Parts 1 and 2. A very rare edition. For part 3 (Venice 1494), see no. 295.
> *Description* in Hain.
> *Collation.* Part 1. [a–z, &, ↄ, ⅌, āb̄⁸ c̄d̄⁶ e–n⁸ o⁶ p¹⁰ q–t⁸ u⁶ xy⁸ z¹⁰ (last leaf gone, blank ?).]
> Part 2. [a–e⁸ f¹² g–m⁸ no⁶ p–x⁸ y⁶ z, &, ↄ, ⅌, a–c⁸ d¹⁰ e–i⁸ kl¹⁰ m–r⁸ s⁶ (last leaf gone).]
> 423 × 286 mm.
> *Binding.* Half-leather with paper sides.
> *Provenance.* Presentation copy to Federigo II da Montefeltro, duke of Urbino (d. Sept. 10, 1482). A vellum leaf, containing the dedication, finely illuminated, is inserted at the beginning of Part 1. The second leaf is also illuminated with the arms of Montefeltro at head, and arms of the author at foot. (Azure a fesse argent between a seated ape *bertuccino*, holding a ring and a star of eight points.)
> The second leaf of Part 2 is also illuminated and has the arms of Duke Federigo at foot. Library bookstamp of Francesco Cardelli of Rome.
> Purchased from Tregaskis, 1902.
> Panzer II. 476 (no. 305). H* 2981.

GEORG HEROLT

286. HIPPOCRATES. De natura hominis etc. [Not after 1484.] 4⁰.

> Dedicated to Pope Sixtus IV (d. 1484).
> *Description* in Hain.
> *Collation.* [a⁸ bc⁶.]

205 × 139 mm.

Binding. Bound with Murray MS. 30 in contemporary Italian binding with 'knot' stamps.

Provenance. Not recorded.

Presented by C. Fairfax Murray, Esq. 1. 905.

HC. *8669. Proctor 3943.

VENICE

FRANZ RENNER, alone

287. SACRO BOSCO (JOHANNES DE). Sphaera Mundi. 1478. 4º.

With the Theorica planetarum of Gerardus Cremonensis, and verses by Franciscus Niger at end.

Description in Hain. Cf. the Morgan Catalogue.

Collation in Morgan and Essling.

Eight woodcut diagrams.

202 × 142 mm.

Binding. Original Italian stamped binding. Clasps wanting. Bound with no. 294; and formerly Alchabitius s. Abdilazi Liber Isagogicus, Ratdolt: Venice, 1482 (Hain* 616), now gone.

Provenance. 'Egerton's auction Major Pearson's copy' MS. note by M. Wodhull, 14 April 1788. Heber II. 3838 (1834). Cornelius Paine (1891), with bookplate.

Purchased for J. and J. Leighton 1891.

H. *14108. Proctor 4175. Morgan 319. Essling 257.

JACQUES LE ROUGE

288. ARETINUS (LEONARDUS). Historia Fiorentina. 12 February 1476. Fº.

Translated by Donato Acciaioli in 1473.

Description in Hain.

Collation. a¹⁰ (a 1 gone, blank?), b–k¹⁰ kk⁶ l–p¹⁰ q¹² r–x¹⁰.

317 × 222 mm. Illuminated capitals from an Italian choir-book pasted in.

Binding. Old vellum.

Provenance. S. M. B. 1784. Edward Davenport, with bookplate.

Purchased, May 1909.

HC. *1562. Proctor 4242.

JOHANN OF COLOGNE AND JOHANN MANTHEN

289. ÆNEAS SYLVIUS. Historia rerum. 1477. Fº.

Description in Hain.

Collation. a–f¹⁰ gh⁸ i–l¹⁰. Wants the first leaf, blank.

270 × 190 mm. Capital at beginning in blue and red. Others in red or blue. Initial strokes in red.

Binding. Calf, with gilt edges (XVIII cent.).

Provenance. Not recorded.

Presented by George Dunn, Esq., May 1909.

HC. *257. Proctor 4322.

290. GRATIANUS. Decretum cum glossa. 3 January 14$\frac{79}{80}$. Fº.

Cum Petri Albigani Trecii prefatione.

Description in Hain.

Collation. a–r¹⁰ s¹² t–z & ꝯ ૪ aa bb¹⁰ cc⁶ dd⁸ ee¹⁰ ff⁸ gg–kk¹⁰ ll⁸ M¹⁰ nn⁸ oo–qq¹⁰ [rr]⁸ (last leaf gone, blank?).

454 × 300 mm. On vellum.

Illustration. Capitals illuminated. At the head of the text on the second leaf a fine vignette of Pope Sixtus IV receiving the book.

Printed in black and red. Paragraph marks in blue or red.

Binding. Red morocco, heavily tooled in gold, by F. Bedford. Gilt edges.

Provenance. Pope Sixtus IV. R. S. Turner[1] (26 June 1888), no. 2271.

Bought from J. and J. Leighton June 1889 by Charles Butler of 3 Connaught Place, who resold it to Leighton, from whom the Museum bought it in 1892.

HC. *7894. Proctor 4338.

ERHARD RATDOLT

WITH B. MALER AND P. LÖSLEIN

291. CEPIO (CORIOLANUS). Mocenici Imperatoris res gestae. 1477. 4º.

Description in Hain and Redgrave.

Illustrations in Redgrave.

Collation in Copinger and Redgrave.

188 × 140 mm. Marginal notes (XVI cent.).

Binding. Stiff paper boards.

Provenance. 'Comes Hercules Silva' (   ) bookstamp. Presented by George Dunn, Esq., May 1909.

HC. *4849. Proctor 4369. Redgrave, *Ratdolt*, 5. Essling 254.

---

[1] See Quaritch's *Book Collectors*, Part VIII.

292. EUSEBIUS. Chronicon. 13 September 1483. 4⁰.

Second edition of St Jerome's Latin translation, with the continuation by
   him, Prosper Aquitanicus, and Matthaeus Palmerius.   At the end the
   epigram of C. Joannes Lucilius Hippodamus Helbronnensis.
For J. L. Santritter.
Description in Hain and Redgrave.
Illustrations in Redgrave.
Collation.   [✳¹² (✳1 gone, blank?)] a–v⁸ x¹⁰.
208 × 148 mm.   Paragraph marks and initial strokes in red
Binding.   Half-calf.
Provenance.   C. G. Raesfeldt, with signature.   Presented by George
   Dunn, Esq., May 1909.
HC. ✳6717.   Proctor 4390.   Redgrave 36.

WENDELIN OF SPEIER

SECOND PRESS

293. DANTE. La divina Comedia. 1477. F⁰.

With the first edition of Boccaccio's Vita di Dante.   The commentary here
   ascribed to Benvenuto da Imola is by Jacopo della Lana.   (See Koch.)
Description in Koch, and Dibdin.
Collation.   [āē⁸ gone] a¹⁰ (a 1, 2 gone) b–k¹⁰ lm⁸ n–s¹⁰ tv⁸ xy¹⁰, aa–gg¹⁰ hh ii⁸,
   ᴋᴋ–ᴏᴏ¹⁰ ᴘᴘ¹² (last gone).
Binding.   Red morocco with the arms and monogram of Prince Eugene of
   Savoy (1663–1736).   See Guigard I. 84.
Provenance.   See above.   Ex libris Friderici de Schennis (armorial book-
   stamp).   Olschki.   Bequeathed by C. Brinsley Marlay, 1912.
HC. 5942.   Proctor 4414.   Dibdin, *Bibl. Spenc.* IV. 105–8.   Koch I. 3–4.

ANTONIUS DE STRATA

AND MARCUS CATANELLUS

294. BLANCHELLUS (MENGHUS), FAVENTINUS. Commentum.
1480. 4⁰.

In Pauli Veneti Logicam.
Description and *Collation* in Copinger.   This copy contains the blan
   first leaf.
202 × 142 mm.
Binding and *Provenance.*   See no. 287.
Copinger II. 1064 = III. 4653.

GEORGIUS ARRIVABENUS

295. BERTACHINUS (JOANNES). Repertorium juris utriusque. 6 November 1494. F⁰.

Part 3. For parts 1 and 2 see no. 285.
Description in Hain.
Collation. [*]⁴, aaa–zzz, &&&, 999, 4 4 4, AAA–MMM⁸ NNN⁶ OOO⁴. 430 × 290 mm. *
Binding. See no. 285.
Provenance. Francesco Cardelli of Rome. Bought with no. 285 in 1902.
H. *2985 (3).

BERNARDINUS RIZUS

296. FORESTI (JACOBUS PHILIPPUS), Bergomensis. Supplementum Chronicarum. 15 May 1490. F⁰.

Description in Hain.
Illustrations. See Essling.
Collation. [*]¹² (first leaf gone, blank?), a–z, &, 9, 4⁸, A–F⁸ G (five leaves only).
308 × 214 mm.
Binding. Pink morocco (early 19th century), gilt tooled. Gilt edges.
Provenance. Syston Park (1884) with bookplates. Purchased from Quaritch 1891.
HC. *2808. Proctor 4954. Essling 343.

MATHEO CAPCASA

297. OVIDIUS. Opera. 31 December 1488. F⁰.

Two volumes (in one).
Description in Hain.
Collation. Vol. I. A–P⁸ Q⁶. Vol. II. a–f⁸ g¹⁰ h–z⁸, &⁸, 9⁴.
Capitals in blue and red. Paragraph marks in red. A few marginal notes (XVI cent.).
Sig. I 6 and 7 have been mutilated.
290 × 191 mm.
Binding. Red morocco, with gilt back, and plain sides.
Provenance. Marlay Bequest, 1912.
H. *12145. Proctor 4988.

PHILIPPUS PINCIUS

298. HORATIUS. Opera cum quattuor commentariis. 13 July 1498. F°.

Description. [Fol. 1.] Horatius cum quat|tuor commentarijs. [Fol. 2.] ❡ Anto. Mancinellus Veliternus *etc.* (Rest as in Copinger.)
Without printer's name. The floriated capital M and the smaller capitals occur in the edition of 1495.
Collation. [✱]², a–z, &, 9, 2+, A–F⁸ G⁶.
Foliated [2], 1–263 (1–cclvii *bis*), 3.
Binding. Red morocco (18th century) with gold tooling.
Provenance. Marlay Bequest, 1912.
Cf. H. 8895. HC. II. 3145 (wanting second leaf).

GIOVANNI CAPCASA

299. HIERONYMUS. Vite di sancti Padri. 4 February 1493. F°.

Ad instantia di Luchantonio di Giunta.
Second edition of the translation attributed to Domenico Cavalca (see Essling).
Description. [Fol. 1 *a.*] Vita di sancti padri vulgare historiata. [1 *b* blank. 2 *a.*] Incominciano le uite de Sancti Padri per diuersi | eloquentissimi Doctori uolgarizate. [Col.] A laude...Venetia per Giouanne dicho de|ca da parma Ad instantia di Luchantonio di Giunta Fiorentino· | ... M.CCCCLXXXXIII. | Adi. ii i (*sic*) di februario...
Illustrations. The compartment on fol. 4 is from the *Supplementum Chronicarum* of 1492. 250 cuts from the *Vite* of 1491. (See Essling.) Inner margin badly wormed.
Collation. a–t⁸ u⁶.
294 × 213 mm.
Binding. Old vellum.
Provenance. T. Kerrich, 1800 with signature. Bequeathed by the Rev. R. E. Kerrich, 1872.
H. 8625. Essling 569.

ALDUS MANUCIUS

300. LASCARIS (CONSTANTINUS). Erotemata. 28 February 149⁴/₅ and 8 March 1495. 4°.

Greek and Latin on opposite pages. With the Pater Noster, Credo, Carmina Aurea Pythagoræ, etc.
The first book printed by Aldus with a date.

Description in Hain.
Collation. a–r^8 s^4, A–C^8.
205 × 142 mm.
Binding. Russia, tooled.
Provenance. W. H. Crawford of Lakelands (1891, lot 1823). Bought at
his sale.
HC. *9924. Proctor 5546.

301. COLONNA (FRANCISCUS).   Poliphili Hypnerotomachia.
December 1499. F^o.

Another copy of no. 140.
Description and *Collation*, see no. 140.
The last leaf of this copy, containing the Errata, in facsimile.
280 × 180 mm.
Binding. Green morocco, with gilt edges, by Zaehnsdorf.
Provenance. Purchased from Quaritch 1891.

302. ——. Another copy.

304 × 210 mm. The initials have been coloured and gilt by a modern hand.
Binding. Dark blue morocco, with plain gold lines (19th century).
Provenance. Library stamp 'O. T. C.' with star of six points. Marlay
Bequest, 1912.

FERRARA

LORENZO ROSSI

303. HIERONYMUS.   Vita e Epistole.   12 October 1497. F^o.

Another state of no. 142. The four preliminary leaves are missing.
At sig. a 1 *b*, in place of the 'Herculis' (cf. Hain and Morgan copy), the
'Eleonoræ' (Paitoni cf. Hain), or the cut of St Jerome of no. 142, is
(within the same border as the above) a woodcut inscription in capitals
'Deo · invisibili · et · immortali · Augustino · Bar|badico · Duci | incly ·
Sena · ppq | veneto · divi | Hiero · episto | hoc volvmen | foelici sydere |
dic · impress· | queest · anno | incar · verbi | MCCCCLXXXXV.'
310 × 209 mm.
Binding. Blue morocco, gilt edges, pink silk linings, by Simier.
Provenance. 'T. Kerrich M.C.C. 1825 July 28th.' Bequeathed by the
Rev. R. E. Kerrich, 1872.

FLORENCE

BARTOLOMMEO DI LIBRI

304. SAVONAROLA. [Epistole a tutti li electi. After 14 August 1497.] 4°.

Description in Copinger and Audin.
Collation. a⁸ b⁶ cd⁸ e⁶ f⁴.
205 × 140 mm.
Illustration. Cuts: (1) on first page, kneeling figure before altar. (2) on sig. b 6 *b*, Crucifixion. (3) on last page the 'Scala Perfectionis.'
Binding. With no. 277. (No. 12 in the volume.)
Provenance. Marlay Bequest, 1912.
HC. 14451. Proctor 6218. Audin 111.

305. SAVONAROLA. Operette. [After 1500?] 4°.

Description in Audin, and Copinger (incorrect).
Collation. a⁴. Cut of crucifixion on first page.
210 × 140 mm.
Binding. With no. 277. (No. 10 in the volume.)
Provenance. Marlay Bequest, 1912.
HC. 14355. Proctor 6304. Audin 41. Reichling III. 173.

LORENZO MORGIANI AND JOHANN PETRI

306. SAVONAROLA. De simplicitate vitae christianae. 28 August 1496. 4°.

Description. (Title) ❡ EPISTOLA FRATER (*sic*) HIERONYMUS | DE FERRARIA ORDINIS PRAE|DICATORUM ['in' *deest*] LIBROS DE | SIMPLICITATE CHRIS-TIA|NAE VITAE | [Cut: a religious writing¹.] Printer's mark on last page.
Collation. a–f⁸.
193 × 124 mm.
Binding. With no. 277.. (No. 8 in the volume.)
Provenance. Marlay Bequest, 1912.
HC. 14357. Proctor 6363. Cf. Audin 52 (with title corrected). Reichling III. 173.

307. SAVONAROLA. Della Simplicita della Vita. 31 October 1496. 4°.

Description. LIBRO | Di frate Hieronymo da Ferrara Della Semplicita | della Vita Christiana Tradocto | IN VOLGARE | [Cut: a religious writing².] Printer's mark on last page.

---

¹ This differs from that in no. 307.   ² This differs from that in no. 306.

Collation. a–e⁸ f¹² g⁸.

210 × 137 mm.

Binding. With no. 277. (No. 7 in the volume.)

Provenance. Marlay Bequest, 1912.

HC. 14358. Proctor 6364. Audin 54.

308. SAVONAROLA. Della Vita Viduale. 26 November 1496. 4°.

Description. ⓒ Comincia illibro della Vita Viduale composto | da frate Hieronymo da Ferrara dellordine de frati predicatori ad instantia & con|templatione di molte diuote Vedo|ue & Vedoui | [Cut: Savonarola preaching to the religious women¹.]

[Colophon on c 3 *b*.] ⓒ IMPRESSO | In Firenze per Ser Lorenzo Morgiani | ad instantia di Ser Piero Pacini | Anno. M.CCCCLXXXXVI | Adi. xxvi. del mese di Nouēbre | [Sig. c 4 *a* blank. Sig. c 4 *b*. Cuts: Lamentation on the dead Christ; and printer's mark.]

Collation. ab⁸ c⁴.

210 × 141 mm.

Binding. With no. 277. (No. 9 in the volume.)

Provenance. Marlay Bequest, 1912.

H. 14370. Audin 51.

309. SAVONAROLA. Expositione del pater noster. [1495.] 4°.

Description. ⓒ La expositione Del pater noster Composta per | Frate Girolamo da Ferrara | [Cut: Agony in the garden, 108 × 85 mm. Christ kneeling to left.]

[Colophon. Cut: Savonarola preaching to the nuns²] FINITA E questa operetta cioe | La expositione del Pater | noster con una epistola auna (*sic*) deuota donna Bolo|gnese Composte da frate Hieronymo de Ferrara | dellordine de frati predicatori |.

Collation. a–c⁸. Several cuts in the text, including the small crucifix cuts as in Audin 29.

•201 × 132 mm.

Binding. With no. 277. (No. 5 in the volume.)

Provenance. Marlay Bequest, 1912.

HC. 14446. Proctor 6397. Audin 28.

310. SAVONAROLA. Expositione del pater noster. [1495.] 4°.

Title. ⓒ La expositione Del pater noster Composta per | Frate Girolamo da Ferrara | [Cut: Agony in the garden.] | ⓒ Prohemio *etc.*

Colophon. [Cut: Reception of nuns.] | FINITA | E | questa operetta cioe | La expositione del Pater | noster con una epistola a una deuota dōna Bolo|gnese Composte da frate Hieronymo da Ferrara | deHordine de frati predicatori.

¹ As in nos. 309 and 310 (Audin 28 and 29).
² As in nos. 310 and 308 (Audin 29 and 51).

Collation. ab⁸ c⁴.   38 lines to the page in sheets a, b; 40 lines to sheet c.
209 × 137 mm.
Cuts. Savonarola and the nuns, differing from the cuts in nos. 308 and 309.
Small crucifix cuts as in Audin 28, but earlier.
Binding. With no. 277.   (No. 2 in the volume.)
Provenance. Marlay Bequest, 1912.
Cf. H. 14445–6.   Cf. Copinger 3298.   Audin 29.

311. SAVONAROLA. Trattato delloratione mentale. [About 1497?] 4°.

Title. ❡ Tractato diuoto & tutto spirituale di frate Hierony|mo da Ferrara dellordine de frati Predicatori in defen|sione & cōmendatione dellora-tione mentale | *etc.* [Cuts: (1) altar and kneeling man and woman. (2) small cut of Christ with book.]
Collation. a⁶ b⁴.
205 × 135 mm.
Binding. With no. 277.   (No. 4 in the volume.)
Provenance. Marlay Bequest, 1912.
Proctor 6399.   Audin 97.

MISCELLANEOUS

312. SAVONAROLA. Trattato dell' umiltà. [After 1500?] 4°.

Description. ❡ Breue & utile tractato della Humilita | composto da | frate Hieronymo da Ferrara dellordine delli | predicatori₊ | [Cut: Christ holding cross.] A cut of the Trinity on sig. a 2; used again in no. 314.
Collation. a¹⁰.
211 × 134 mm.
Binding. With no. 277.   (No. 1 in the volume.)
Provenance. Marlay Bequest, 1912.
HC. 14375.   Proctor 6447.   Audin 57.

313. SAVONAROLA. Sermone della oratione a M. A. d. S. [After 1500?] 4°.

Description. ❡ Sermone della oratione a. M₊A₊d₊S₊ composto da frate | Hieronymo da Ferrara dellordine de frati predicatori ₊ Prohemio ₊ [Cut: Agony in the Garden : Christ kneeling to right.   Plain edge¹.]
Collation. a⁸ b⁴.   Lombardic capitals in the text (as no. 314).
210 × 139 mm.
Binding. With no. 277.   (No. 3 in the volume.)
Provenance. Marlay Bequest, 1912.
HC. *14403.   Proctor 6446.   Audin 93.

¹ This differs from the cut in no. 309 (Audin 28).

314. SAVONAROLA.   Operetta del amore di Jesu.   [After 1500?]   4°.

Description.   ❦ Operetta del amore di Jesu Composta da | frate Hieronymo
da Ferrara. | . ✠. ⊰ [Cut: Crucifixion in plain border.]   Title in black
letter.   Text in roman letter with Lombardic capitals (as no. 313).   A
small Crucifixion on f. 17.   At foot of the last page is the cut of the
Trinity used in no. 312.

Collation.   ab⁸ c⁶.

211 × 138 mm.

Binding.   With no. 277.   (No. 6 in the volume.)

Provenance.   Marlay Bequest, 1912.

HC. *14348.   Proctor 6448.   Audin 38.

TREVISO

BERNHARD OF COLOGNE

315. SENECA.   Opera.   1478.   F°.

Second edition.

Description in Hain.

Collation in Copinger.   This copy wants first and last leaves, both blank.

320 × 215 mm.   Capitals, initial letters and paragraph marks in blue or red.
Some marginal notes (XVI cent.).

Binding.   Olive morocco, gilt edges, by W. Pratt.

Provenance.   W. H. Crawford of Lakelands (1891, lot 2860) with bookplate.
Presented by George Dunn, Esq., May 1909.

HC. *14591.   Proctor 6484.

MANTUA

JOHANN SCHALL

316. EUSEBIUS.   Historia Ecclesiastica.   July 1479.   F°.

The Latin translation by Rufinus.   Fourth edition.

Description in Hain.

Collation.   [a–s⁸ t⁶ v⁸ x⁶ y⁸ (y 8 gone).}

298 × 205 mm.   First page only rubricated.

Binding.   Green half-calf.

Provenance.   'Sancte Anōtiate Eremj ad usum fratris Lucretii de Medulis'
and 'Ordinis fratrum eremitarum S. Augⁿⁱ observantie L.......'   Comes
Hercules Silva (bookstamp).   George Dunn (bookplate).

Presented by George Dunn, Esq., May 1909.

HC. *6711.   Proctor 6908.

VERONA
JOHANNES OF VERONA

317. VALTURIUS (ROBERTUS). De re militari. 1472. F°.
Another copy of no. 156.
Description and *Collation.* See no. 156.
325 × 230 mm. White vine capitals, and smaller capitals in blue. No
written chapter headings. Some marginal notes (XVI cent.).
Very imperfect copy, wanting 133 leaves.
Binding. Modern vellum.
Provenance. Not known.
Purchased, 1891.

PIERRE MAUFER

318. JOSEPHUS. Opera. 25 December 1480. F°.
Second dated edition of the Latin translation.
Description in Hain. (Two preliminary leaves there described seem never
to have been in this copy, which begins with a blank leaf.)
Collation. a¹⁰ [a 1 blank not signed, the second leaf signed a 1] b⁸ c⁶ d–k,
kk, l–x⁸ y⁶, A–C⁸ D⁶.
On sig. a 5 b the last six words of sig. a 5 have been repeated by accident.
285 × 195 mm. Not rubricated. A few marginal notes in the first four quires.
Binding. Vellum (XVIII cent.).
Provenance. Archinto (1863) with bookplate. Presented by George Dunn, Esq.,
May 1909.
HC. *9452. Proctor 6918. Morgan II. 179 (no. 471).

BRESCIA
BONINUS DE BONINIS

319. DANTE. La divina comedia. 31 May 1487. F°.
With Landino's commentary.
Another copy of no. 158.
Collation and *Description.* See no. 158. The first leaf is made up. Wants
last leaf blank.
343 × 224 mm.
Binding. Red morocco by M. Lortic. Gilt edges.
Provenance. Bought from L. S. Olschki, Florence, January 1907 (no. 2040
in his catalogue of that date). Bequeathed by C. Brinsley Marlay, 1912.

SWITZERLAND

BASLE

MICHAEL WENSSLER

With Bernhard Richel[1]

320. CARRACIOLUS (ROBERTUS). Sermones Quadragesimales. 1475. Fº.

> *Description* in Hain and BM. Catalogue.
> *Collation* in BM. Catalogue. In this copy leaves 1–16 (the table) are bound at the end.
> 287 × 210 mm. Rubricated. Capitals in plain red.
> *Binding*. Original stamped pigskin with metal bosses and clasps. A 12th century MS. fragment on vellum at the end.
> *Provenance*. The Dominican House at Ratisbon (bookplate). Cornelius Paine (1891) with bookplate. Purchased from J. and J. Leighton, 1891.
> H. *4432. Proctor 7462=7525. BM. Catalogue III. 736 (cf. 722).

321. MANDEVILLE (JOHANNES). Reisen nach Hierusalem. [About 1482?] Fº.

> German translation by Otto von Diemeringen.
> *Description* in Brunet and Copinger.
> *Collation*. ab¹⁰ c⁸ d⁸ (+4* het er den) e–g⁸ hi⁶ k–m¹⁰; 103 leaves. Wants a 1, i 1 and m 10; g 5 and h 5 mutilated.
> Mr F. Jenkinson supplies the following note :
> 'This book is printed in the types 5, 6, 7 used by B. Richel in Hugo de Sancto Caro, Postilla, at Basle in 1482 (Proctor 7537). But the lower case h of type 6 differs entirely, and has not yet been identified. What happened to Richel's type after his press stopped in that year? It is possible that J. Besicken and Peter Kollicker may have carried on the press. (Cf. Proctor 7652–3.)'
> *Illustration*. 143 cuts, coloured. These differ from those used by Hupfuff at Strassburg in 1501. (Cf. Morgan Catalogue, 71.)
> Arms of Basle on fol. 45.

---

[1] Cf. Hain *4432.

Binding. German half-binding.

Provenance. Georg Kloss (1835), with bookplate. Earl of Ashburnham (1897), lot 2465. Purchased from Ellis and Elvey, 1898.

Cf. H. 10646. Brunet Supplement I. 931. Copinger 3833. Cf. Woolley Facsimiles 351 (Proctor 7537). Schreiber 4799.

MICHAEL FURTER

322. VEGIUS (MAFFEUS). Philalethes. [About 1490.] 4°.

Description in Hain.

Collation. ab⁸.

211 × 153 mm. Cut and capital letter coloured yellow.

Binding. Paper boards.

Provenance. Cornelius Paine (1891), with bookplate. Purchased from J. and J. Leighton, 1891.

HC. *15927. Proctor 7644. Morgan I. 238 (no. 230. Cf. no. 49). BM. Catalogue III. 782.

FRANCE

PARIS

JEAN DU PRÉ

323. BREVIARIUM Magnum ad usum Parisiensem. 9 June 1492. F°.

Printed in agreement with the booksellers Guillaume Caron and Jean Belin (Claudin).

Description in Copinger.

Illustration. Cuts from a Horae. Some coloured.

Collation. [✳]⁸, ✠⁸, A–H⁸ IK⁶, AABB⁸ CC¹⁰, a–e⁸ f⁶, āē⁸ ī¹⁰, aa–ff⁸ gg⁶ hh–tt⁸ vv xx⁶.

333 × 236 mm. Capital and initial letters in red and blue.

Binding. Russia, with yellow edges, with Wodhull bookstamp.

Provenance. Over the half-title and at commencement of text the word 'Chateau' (XVI cent.).

M. Wodhull. Richard, Viscount Fitzwilliam, with signature, 1808. Fitzwilliam Bequest, 1816.

HC. 3869. Claudin, *Histoire* I. 261.

PIERRE LE ROUGE

324. LA MER DES Histoires. 1488. F°.

For the attribution to Jean Colonna see Brunet s.v. Rudimentum Noviciorum. Printed for Vincent Commin.

Description in Brunet and Copinger.

Illustrations. Cuts and metal borders. See Claudin.

Collation. Vol. I. [✳]⁴, a⁸ (gone), a–z, &, aa–gg⁸ hh¹⁰ (last leaf gone).

Vol. II. A–X, AA–MM⁸ NN¹⁰, āē⁸ īō⁶, ss⁸.

400 × 290 mm. Capitals and paragraph marks in red and blue. Initial strokes in yellow.

Binding. Red morocco, gilt edges. (Chambolle-Duru, 1866.)

Provenance. Purchased (through Deighton and Bell), 1890.

Copinger 3991. Proctor 8092. Claudin, *Histoire* I. 458 etc.

325. BOCCACCIO. Genealogie des dieux. 9 February 1498. F⁰.

First edition of the French translation. The translator not known (see
  Fairfax Murray).
Printed for A. Verard.
Description in Copinger, Macfarlane and Morgan.
Illustrations. See Macfarlane and Murray.
Collation. a–z, &, 9, AB⁸ CD⁶ E⁴.
355 × 247 mm.
Binding. Brown morocco, gilt edges, by Chambolle-Duru.
Provenance. Purchased from J. and J. Leighton, 1893.
HC. 3325.   Macfarlane 56.   Pellechet 2471.   Morgan II. 243 (no. 536).
  C. Fairfax Murray, *Early French Books* I. 37 (no. 47).

PHILIPPE PIGOUCHET

326. HEURES à l'usage de' Rome. 20 August 1496. 4⁰.

Printed for S. Vostre.   The earliest edition in which the 'Dance of Death'
  occurs.
Description in Hain.
Illustrations. Metal-cut borders and 16 full-page illustrations. F. 36, on
  which is one of the cuts, is in facsimile.   Capitals in gold.   Smaller
  capitals in blue or red.   Four cuts are coloured and have burnished
  gold frames.
Collation. a–k⁸ l⁴, A⁸.
220 × 153 mm.
Binding. Dark brown morocco, gilt tooled (French, XVI cent.).   Rebacked,
  gilt edges.
Provenance. Purchased from J. and J. Leighton, May 1893.
HC. 8851.   Proctor 8187.   Brunet v. 1579 (no. 28).   Lacombe 36.   Bohatta 545.

327. HORAE ad usum Sarum. 16 May 1498. 8⁰.

On vellum.   Printed for S. Vostre.
Description. [Sig. a 1.] Hore presentes ad vsum Sarum impresse fuerūt
  Pa|risiis per Philippū pigouchet Anno salutis. M.CCCC. | XCVIII. die vero.
  xvi. Maii pro Symone Vostre: librario | cōmorante ibidē: in vico nuncu-
  pato nouo beate Marie in | intersignio sancti Johannis evaṅgeliste.
  [Pigouchet's mark above.]
Illustrations. Each page within made-up metal border.   The large cuts
  occur in other editions printed by Pigouchet.   Gold capital on red or
  blue ground.
Collation. abc⁸ (c 7 gone) de⁸ (e 2 and 3 gone) f⁶ g–l⁸ (l 2 and 3 gone) m–q⁸.
179 × 106 mm.
Binding. Mottled calf (XVIII cent.).

Provenance. Signature of Jarvis Kenrick on verso of first leaf and again on
sig. e 5 *b*.   T. Kerrich, 'MCC. 1791.'
Bequeathed by the Rev. R. E. Kerrich, 1872.
H. 8863.   Proctor 8194.   S. Sandars, *Vellum Books.*   Hoskins 17.

ULRICH GERING

With B. Rembolt

328.   GREGORIUS.   Expositio super cantica.   16 January
1498⁄9.   4º.

Third edition.
Description in Hain-Copinger.
Collation.   a–c⁸ d⁶.
203 × 134 mm.   Not rubricated.
Binding.   Modern vellum.
Provenance.   Presented by George Dunn, Esq., May 1909.
HC. 7939.   Proctor 8309.

SUCCESSOR OF E. JEHANNOT

329.   HEURES à l'usage de Rome.   20 Janvier 1500.   8º.

On vellum.   No general title.   Printed by Jean Poiterin or Le Dru.   (See
Proctor II. 597.)   For A. Verard (Bohatta).
Description in Copinger.
Collation.   Aa⁸ Bb¹⁰, a–i⁸ k⁴, A–D⁸ ; 126 leaves.
180 × 114 mm.
Illustrations.   Variety of Pigouchet's second set (Murray).
Binding.   Modern green morocco.
Provenance.   Bought about 1891? (qu. from Cohn?).
Copinger II. 3102.   Bohatta 624.   Cf. C. Fairfax Murray, *Early French
Books* I. 289.

HOLLAND

GOUDA
GERARDUS LEEU

330.　Dialogus Creaturarum Moralizatus.　31 August 1482.　Fᵒ.

Second edition.　For the first edition, see no. 175.

Description in Campbell.

Illustrations.　See Conway.

Collation.　[aa⁴ bb⁶ gone], a⁸ (a 1 gone) bc⁸ (c 6 and 8 gone) d⁸ (d 1 and 8 gone) e⁸ (e 1, 4, and 7 gone) f⁸ (f 4 and 5 gone) g⁸ (g 3, 6-8 gone) h⁸ (h 4 and 5 gone 6 mutilated) i⁸ (i 8 gone) k⁸ (k 7 gone) l⁸ (l 3-5 gone) m⁶. Sig. h 6 and k 6, m 4 and 5, are from a copy of the first edition.

273 × 195 mm.

Binding.　Half-calf, paper sides (XVIII cent.).

Provenance.　R. Farmer (1798), with signature.

Purchased 1891.

HC. 6127.　CA. *562.　Conway, p. 330.

ZWOLLE
PIETER VAN OS
Second Press

331.　BERNARDUS.　Sermones in Duytsche.　27 May 1495.　Fᵒ.

Description in Campbell.

Illustrations.　See Conway.

Collation.　1⁴, a–y, A–G⁶ H⁴ IK⁶ L⁴ M–Y⁶, A⁶ B⁴ C⁶ (C 2-5 gone).

277 × 200 mm.　Capitals in red.

Binding.　Fine contemporary brown leather with panelled sides and blind tooling.　Modern clasps.

Provenance.　Inscription inside the upper cover: 'Dit boeck hoort tot die clarissen binnen Mechelen.'　T. Kerrich 'MCC. June 5, 1827.'　Bequeathed by the Rev. R. E. Kerrich, 1872.

HC. 2854.　CA. *276.　Proctor 9145.　Conway, pp. 337-8.

BELGIUM

LOUVAIN

JOHANN OF PADERBORN

332. CICERO. De officiis. [About 1483.] F°.

Cum Petri Marsi interpretatione. See Erasmus, *Epistolae*, ed. P. S. Allen,
I. 356 n.
Description in Campbell, and Hain-Copinger.
Collation. a⁸ (a 1 blank gone) b–z, A–I⁸ K¹⁰.
279 × 188 mm. Pin-holes throughout. Marginal notes (XVI cent.). On the
flyleaves in the same hand are copies of the two letters by Erasmus to
Jacobus Tutor, dated 4 Id. Sept. 1519 and 4 Cal. Mai. 1488, printed in
P. S. Allen's edition of the Epistolae.
Binding. Brown calf (XVIII cent.). With nos. 333 and 334.
Provenance. J. E. Millard (1890) with bookplate. Purchased for J. and
J. Leighton, 1891.
HC. 5269. CA. *438. Proctor 9232.

333. CICERO. Paradoxa. [About 1483.] F°.

Cum Petri Marsi interpretatione.
Description in Campbell.
Collation. a⁸ bc⁶.
279 × 198 mm.
Binding and *Provenance.* See no. 332.
CA. *445. Proctor 9231 (2).

334. CICERO. De Amicitia et de Senectute. 17 May 1483. F°.

Description in Hain, Campbell.
Collation. a–c⁸ d¹⁰.
279 × 198 mm.
Binding and *Provenance.* See no. 332.
HC. 5272. CA. *433. Proctor 9231.

ANTWERP
GERARDUS LEEU

335. FRANCISCUS (MICHAEL) DE INSULIS. Speculum ser-
monum. 2 August 1487. 4º.

The only edition of this work.
Description in Campbell.
Illustration. Woodcut on title. See Conway.
Collation. a–l⁶ (last leaf, with printer's mark, gone).
205 × 141 mm.
Binding and *Provenance.* See no. 270. (No. 1 in the volume.) Purchased,
    1891, lot 2976 at the W. H. Crawford sale.
HC. 7349. CA. *1576. Proctor 9366. Conway, p. 330.

336. LIBELLUS de modo confitendi. 12 Kal. Martii, 1488. 4º.

Description in Copinger.
Collation. a–c⁶ d⁸ (last leaf gone, blank).
205 × 141 mm.
Binding and *Provenance.* See no. 270. (No. 4 in the volume.) Purchased,
    1891, lot 2976 at the W. H. Crawford sale.
HC. 11498 (this copy). CA. 1134+.

CLAES LEEU

337. COLLOQUIUM peccatoris et Christi. 17 May 1488. 4º.
Description in Campbell.
Collation. ab⁶ c⁴.
205 × 141 mm. Rubricated.
Binding and *Provenance.* See no. 270. (No. 2 in the volume.) Purchased,
    1891, lot 2976 at the W. H. Crawford sale.
CA. *466. Proctor 9431. Morgan III. 129–130 (no. 652).

GHENT
AREND DE KEYSERE

338. BOETHIUS. De philosophiae consolatione. 3 May
1485. Fº.

In Latin and Flemish with Flemish annotations.
Description in Campbell.

Illustrations. Parti-coloured capitals and paragraph marks. Underlinings in red. Large illuminations at the beginning of each book[1].

Collation. a⁶ (a 1 gone, blank) b⁶, a–z, &, A–M⁸ N–R⁸ ST⁶ V⁸ (V 8 gone, blank).

359 × 251 mm.

Binding. Elaborate modern stamped pigskin with metal bosses and clasps.

Provenance. Exhibited in the Paris Exhibition of 1880. Purchased, 1892.

HC. 3400. Cf. CA. *322. Proctor 9461.

---

[1] The coloured illustrations in the Colard Mansion edition in the Cambridge University Library bear a striking resemblance.

LIST OF ILLUSTRATED BOOKS

Æsopus. Vita et fabulae. Knoblochtzer, Strassburg. [1481?] F°. **25.**
Albertus Magnus. De misterio missae. J. Zainer, Ulm. 1477. F°. **102.**
Alfonsus. Tabulae Astronomicae. Ratdolt, Venice. 1483. 4°. **125.**
Apianus. Astronomicon. Apianus, Ingolstadt. 1540. F°. **188.**
—— Quadrans Astronomicus. Ibid. 1532. F°. **187.**
Ariosto. Orlando Furioso. V. Valgrisi, Venice. 1571. 4°. **230.**
Aristoteles. Opera. Aldus, Venice. 1495. F°. **138.**
Astronomici Veteres. Opera. Aldus, Venice. 1499. F°. **139.**
Augustinus. Canones. Schott, Strassburg. 1490. F°. **27.**

Bayer (J.). Uranometria. C. Mangus, Augsburg. 1603. F°. **182.**
Berlinghieri. Geographia. N. Laurentii, Florence. [1481.] F°. **148.**
Bernardus. Sermones. P. van Os, Zwolle. 1495. F°. **331.**
Biblia Germanica. A. Koberger, Nuremberg. 1483. F°. **93.**
Biblia Latina. L. A. de Giunta, Venice. 1519. 8°. **214.**
Biringucchio. De la Pirotechnia. V. Roffinello, Venice. 1540. 4°. **221.**
Boccaccio. Genealogie. P. le Rouge, Paris. 1498. F°. **325.**
—— Erlychten Frouen. J. Prüss, Strassburg. 1488. F°. **268.**
Boethius. De Consolatione. J. Grüninger, Strassburg. 1501. F°. **190, 191.**
Botho (C.). Chronik. Schoeffer, Mainz. 1492. F°.
Bradwardine (T.). Arithmetica. J. Joffré, Valencia. 1503. F°. **253.**
Brant (S.). Stultifera Navis. J. B. de Olpe, Basel. 1498. 4°. **167.**
Breydenbach. Itinerarium. E. Renwich, Mainz. 1486. F°. **263.**
—— Reise. Ibid. 1486. F°. **9.**
Brigitta. Revelationes. A. Koberger, Nuremberg. 1500. F°. **280.**
Bry (J. T. and J. I. de). Petits Voyages. Pt v. M. Becker, Frankfort. 1601. F°. **184.**
—— —— vi. W. Richter, ibid. 1603. F°. **185.**
—— —— vii. W. Richter, ibid. 1606. F°. **186.**
Bry (T. de). America. Pt iv. Frankfort. 1594. F°. **183.**
Buchlein von Leben unsers Herrn. A. Sorg, Augsburg. 1491. F°. **276.**

Caoursin (G.). Obsidio Rhodiae. J. Reger, Ulm. 1496. F°. **283.**
Cepio. Mocenici Imperatoris res gestae. E. Ratdolt, Venice. 1477. 4°. **291.**
Chronik der Sachsen. Schoeffer, Mainz. 1492. F°. **7.**
Chroniques de France. J. Maurand, Paris. 1493. F°. **171.**
Colonna. Hypnerotomachia. Aldus, Venice. 1499. F°. **302.**
Cosmographiae Introductio. J. A. de Nicolinis, Venice. 1535. 8°. **219.**

Dante. Comedia. B. de Boninis, Brescia. 1487. F°. **158, 319.**
—— —— P. de Piasiis, Venice. 1491. F°. **127.**
—— —— A. Paganini, Toscolano. [1502?] 8°. **203.**
—— —— B. Stagnino, Venice. 1512. 4°. See **216.**
—— —— B. Stagnino, Venice. 1520. 4°. **215, 216.**
—— —— A. Paganini, Toscolano. [1527?] 8°. **203.**
—— —— J. del Burgofranco for L. A. Giunta, Venice. 1529. F°. **217.**
—— —— F. Marcolini, Venice. 1544. 4°. **222.**
Dialogus Creaturarum. G. Leeu, Gouda. 1480. F°. **175.**
—— —— G. Leeu, Gouda. 1482. F°. **330.**
Durandus (G.). Rationale. J. Zainer, Ulm. 1473. F°. **103.**

Euclides. Elementa. E. Ratdolt, Venice. 1482. F°. **121.**
—— —— J. Tacuinus, Venice. 1505. F°. **205.**
Eusebius. Chronicon. E. Ratdolt, Venice. 1483. 4°. **292.**

Foresti. De claris mulieribus. L. Rossi, Ferrara. 1497. F°. **141.**
—— Supplementum. B. Benalius, Venice. 1486. F°. **131, 131 A.**
—— —— B. Rizus, Venice. 1490. F°. **296.**
Franciscus de Insulis. Speculum. G. Leeu, Antwerp. 1487. 4°. **335.**

Geiler. Keiserspergs Passion. J. Reinhard, Strassburg. 1513. F°. **193.**
Geldenhaur (G.). De terrifico cometa. J. Knoblouch, Strassburg. 1508. 4°. **195.**
Guido Bonatus. Astrologia. E. Ratdolt, Augsburg. 1491. 4°. **85.**
Guido de Columnis. Historie. Schott, Strassburg. 1489. F°. **26.**

Heures. *See* Horae.
Hieronymus. Vite di sancti padri. G. Capcasa, Venice. 1493. F°. **299.**
—— Vita e Epistole. L. Rossi, Ferrara. 1497. F°. **142, 303.**
Hondius (J.). Italiae Descriptio. B. et A. Elzeviri, Leiden. 1627. F°. **248.**
Horae (F.). P. Pigouchet for S. Vostre. Paris. 20 Aug. 1496. 4°. **326.**
—— (L.). P. Pigouchet for S. Vostre. Paris. 16 May 1498. 8°. **327.**
—— (F.). For A. Verard. Paris. 20 Jan. 1500. 8°. **329.**
—— (F.). P. Pigouchet for G. Eustace. Paris. 1509. 8°. **233.**
—— (L.). T. Kerver. Paris. 1519. 8°. **238.**
—— (E.). T. Petyt. London. [153-.] 16°. **254.**
—— (F.). J. Kerver. Paris. 1558. 8°. **242.**
Horatius. Opera. J. Reinhard, Strassburg. 1498. F°. **29.**
Hyginus. Poeticon Astronomicon. T. de Blavis, Venice. 1488. 4°. **129.**

Isidorus. Etymologiae. Mentelin, Strassburg. [1473.] F°. **16.**

Jacobus de Theramo. Belial. C. Fyner, Esslingen. [1475?] F°. **101.**
Jacopone da Todi. Laude. F. Buonaccorsi, Florence. 1490. 4°. **152.**
Johannes Junior. Scala Coeli. J. Eber, Strassburg. 1483. F°. **30.**
Justinianus. Codex. J. Sensenschmid and A. Frisner, Nuremberg. 1475. F°. **95.**

Keyerslach (P.). Passio Christi. Zell, Cologne. [1495.] 4°. **52.**

Plate I

amicū qȝ inimicū habes:Cui in ciuitate inſidias fe
ciſti acillaes. quo iure cū de exilio tuo duaco ediſti
eum ſequeris.quos tyrannos appellabas: Eoꝛ po
tentie faues qui tibi ante optiates videbanͤ .eoſdͤ
dementes et furioſos vocas:Vatini cauſam agis. de
ſeſtro male exiſtimas bibulū petulantiſſimis verb
leͦ. laudas ceſarem qȝ maxime odiſti.ei maxime
obſequeris:Alͦ ſtans alio ſedens ſentis de ſi. P.
hijs maledicis.illos odiſti leuiſſime transfuga neȝ
in hac.neqȝ in illa parte fidem habes:

Reſponſio.M.T.Ciceronis contra in
uectiuā.G.Saluſtij

N demū magna voluptas ē.G.Saluſti
ac qualem ac parem verbis vitam agere
nec quitȝ tam obſcenum dicere cui non
ab initio puericie omnū generi ſactoꝛis etas tua re
ſpondeat.vt omis ratio moribȝ conſonȝ: Neqȝ ein
qui ita viuit vt tu.ahter ac tu loqui poteſt Neqȝ q̄
tam illeto ſermone vtitur ei vita honeſtioꝛ eſſe po
terit: Quo me vertam pꝛes cariſſimi.vn inciū ſu
mā. maius ein in dicendi onus imponiͭ q̄ notioꝛ
eſt vterqȝ nͤm: Qd ſi aut de mea vita atqȝ actibo
huic conuiciatoi eſpodeo.inuidia gliaꝛ cōleᵗ Aut ſi
h⁹fcā moͤs oͤȝ etatē nudauͤo.ī idē viciū iauoāꝑea
citatis qd huic obicio At vos ſi forte offedimi iuſti⁹
huic q̄ in ſuccenſere debeatis qui inciū introduxit

No. 58.   Sallustius, Invectiva.   Cologne, about 1470

Plate II

wider das·das der Helleal ander
selben clage benempt vnd gemelt
hat Nun sol Moyses mit den zúge
wisen die da benempt sint vor vns
da von so gebieten vnd empfelhen
wir dir ernschlich das du den nach
geschriben zúgen fúrbietest chef:
tiglich das sie des nesten tags nach
dem fúr gebot vor vns Jn vnserm
huß gegenwerttiglich hrē vñ sagen
was Jn kunt vnd wissen hy vmb
das·das wir sie werden frage ouch
soltu etzff iglich fúr bietrn dem bel
leal der helle verweser das er ouch
an dem selben tag gegenwirtiglich
hy vnd sehe die zúgen vnd hóre ir
Eyde die hy vmb ire zúgkmisse sagē
vnd schweren werden vnd das er
verantwúrt die fúrlegung vñ stu
ck die Moyses fúr das gericht het
geleit durch wisung willen smer
Rechte dem búte also fúr vnd laß
vns dz her wider wissen Datū des
andern tags des abrellen. Vt pf
detesti. Jn·nōīe·dūi·⁊·detesti·c·j·
⁊·iij. Die zúgen smd also genant.
Abraham· Isaac· Jacop· Dauid·
Johanes·der·tóuffer· Aristotiles·
Virgilius·vnd· Ipocras·

Je zúgkmisse wart gela:
den vñ dē Richterwart
das kunt geton vnd vff
den gesatzten tag satz si:
ch der Richter vff den gericht stúl
Alß gewonlich ist vnd ward den
zúgen gerúfft Als den sytt vnd ge:
wonheit ist da warent sy engēgen
vnd der Helleal mit jnen da wart
der belleal gefragt was er gestún:
de an den stucken der fúrlegunge
Moysi das wolt Helleal mit ver:
antwúrten·

Abies jne der Richter
antwúrten vñ do besor
gt sich belleal ob er Jm
mit antwirt gebe so wúr
de von des rechts wegen geschatz
er gestúnd synem wider teil vñ he:
me also von synem rechten. Vt·de
affelß·c·v·li°·vj· vnd dar vmb gab
er antwúrt vnd sprach er gestún:
de Der fúrlegung vnd stucke Die
Moyses het fúr geleit etlichs vnd
etlichs mit vß genomen das zú dem
ersten das die hellisch gemeind der

La primeramente los que oyen la musica:alcançan los puechos:que hauemos dicho: mas no los musicos mismos.La(segū dize Aristoteles) lo que hōbre oye mueue mas que lo sensible:o lo que obra por si Ante segun el mismo por la fuerça τ muchidūbre de vozes: se danya el celebro. τ se danyan essomismo los spiritus vitales delos cantores.de lo ql se sigue que se tornan mal dispuestos pa los buenos costūbres alos quales llama Aristoteles indispuestos para las cosas del ingenio. Otrosi la musica τ el vso de aqlla:por ciertas melodias dispone a amollecer el anio:τ algunas veses a saña. τ otras cosas diuersas: que apartan al hōbre dela virtud τ

delas obras del entēdimiēto por lo ql alos viejos: τ grādes: τ studiosos varones les mādan oir la musica: τ iudgar ō aqlla:mas no poner la por obra. La es cosa cōueniēte: (segū dizē los sauios)q el varō graue no solamēte a parte las manos mas aū la voz ōla musica pa q otros no le burlē por q aqllo es cosa de truhanes. Añade a esto:lo q to caremos abaxo enel.ij. libro enel capitulo.xv.endonde tractaremos delos chātres.

Capitulo.xl.dela.iij.τ.iiij. arte mechanica:es a saber dela Arismetica:τ geometria. τ de los loores τprouecho dellas τ delos incōuenientes τ trabajos dellas.

A Arismetica:τ Geometria sō las postreras artes mechanicas τ son

muy puechosas. La vna delas qles tracta delos cuētos: τ la otra ō qntitades τ grādezas:en las qua   b iiij

Plate IV

No. 14.   Augustinus, Confessiones.   Strassburg, about 1470

Plate V

No. 43.   Caracciolus de Licio, Sermones quadragesimales.   Cologne, 1473

Plate VI

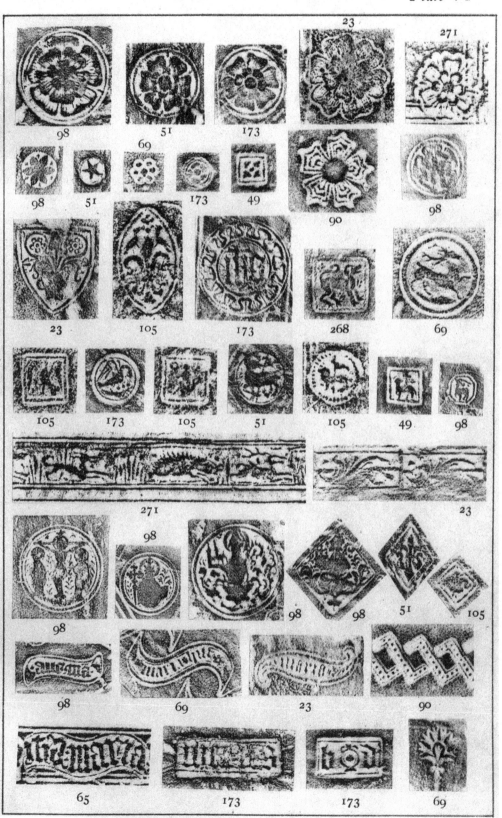

Stamps on Mediaeval bindings

INDEX

Bookplates. BOOK NO.

Cambridge:
PRINTED BY J. B. PEACE, M.A.,
AT THE UNIVERSITY PRESS

Printed in the United States
By Bookmasters